Marion Howard

Maggie's rosary and other tales

Marion Howard

Maggie's rosary and other tales

ISBN/EAN: 9783741163258

Manufactured in Europe, USA, Canada, Australia, Japa

Cover: Foto ©Andreas Hilbeck / pixelio.de

Manufactured and distributed by brebook publishing software (www.brebook.com)

Marion Howard

Maggie's rosary and other tales

MAGGIE'S ROSARY,

AND

OTHER TALES.

BY THE AUTHOR OF "MARION HOWARD."

EDITED BY MRS. WASHINGTON HIBBERT,
AND DEDICATED TO HER GRANDCHILDREN.

LONDON:
BURNS, OATES, AND COMPANY,
17, PORTMAN STREET, AND 63, PATERNOSTER ROW.

CONTENTS.

	PAGE
MAGGIE'S ROSARY .	. 1
THE WHITE ANGEL .	15
MABEL .	. 49
OLD MORGAN'S ROSE-TREE .	87

PREFACE.

THE writer of these charming stories has requested I would do her the favour to edit them. Believing that the Catholic world of little children would be a great loser if they were not published, I gladly do so. No one who has read the beautiful tale of "Marion Howard" can doubt that any book by the same pen, expressly written, as these little stories are, for little children, will both interest and benefit them. The writer possesses in an eminent degree the art of making stories for children. Though she writes like one who is fully aware that books for children must contain a sufficient amount of the element of amusement in order to be read, her stories, which are by no means wanting in amusement, owe their chief excellence to the fact that they aim at something more. To supply books for children or grown-up people who read to kill time or banish trouble from the mind, is no part of her design in anything that she has written; rather quite the contrary, and every mother and grandmother, like myself, ought to be grateful to any one who comes forward to write books as the Author does, which do not create in the minds of young people that diseased, ruinous appetite for sensational reading now so fearfully prevalent, and so strongly condemned by our Holy Father Pope Pius the Ninth. The foundation of the Catholic woman, the Author rightly assumes, as our own experience also tells us, is laid in the child while the schoolroom and the nursery are its whole world. There and then the habits, the tastes, the likings and dislikings which make the grown-up man or woman, are in their budding stage. The course pursued by the Author, of teaching the little boys and girls who figure in her pieces to have direct recourse for relief to religion in their little fallings and failings, is what our ever to be remembered and venerated Cardinal Wiseman set an example of, in his beautiful tale " Fabiola," and, among the last gifts of his pen to us, in his celebrated lecture on " Mental Culture."

Many people think that little children ought not to be taught to test their little every-day acts as grown-up people are called upon to do, by an appeal to religion and conscience; but I am glad to say that in the following stories everything is opposed to that view. The child which has been given to God in baptism, and which has thereby been made a child of God, can only be taught to square its acts by one standard, and that the will of God, who has made Himself its Father. The Author shows how this divine principle may be practically applied, and how it succeeded within her own experience with children who were reared under her management. As the "war cry" of the day and of Satan is, "Let religion be shut out of schools," it becomes a matter of greater care and anxiety to us all to give and encourage only such teaching to the young as will accord with their higher destination as the children of God, while they are, as the children of earthly parents, being instructed in those things which will fit them for their lower condition on earth. I hope there will be so great a demand for this little book that the amiable and talented author will now and then send forth, as time goes on, a few more books of the kind.

JULIA M. M. WASHINGTON HIBBERT.

12, HILL STREET, BERKELEY SQUARE,
15*th December*, 1871.

MAGGIE'S ROSARY,

AND

OTHER TALES.

MAGGIE'S ROSARY.

Two little girls were standing together in a quiet street, chatting very busily. They had just come from school, and had more books, and slates, and music to carry than their not very strong arms could well manage. But it was getting so near the grand examination that they expected a little more work, and consequently a little more to carry, and they were too gay in anticipation of their prizes to grumble.

"Maggie," said the younger one, "you told me just before school that you had something to show me. What is it?"

"Guess."

"A doll?"

"A doll! Minnie! Fancy a girl of twelve

years old having a doll!" and Maggie seemed to grow at least two inches taller. "We have quite enough to do at home, with looking after live dolls, I can tell you, without taking to wax ones."

"Well, then, a new dress?"

"No, I wish it was, then poor mamma wouldn't have to buy me one this spring. You must guess again."

"I give it up. I might guess everything from a gold watch down to a kitten, and yet be wrong every time. What is it?"

"Josephine Mason's portrait. It came in a letter this morning."

"Is that all?" asked Minnie, in a disappointed tone. "But I daresay you are glad, for you were such great friends. Is it like her?"

"See," said Maggie, taking it out of her geography.

Both were soon very intent on examining it, and many were their criticisms on the eyes, nose, mouth, and dress of the pretty little girl represented in the *carte*.

"I will show you her letter," said Maggie; "she sent you her love in it."

Here began a vast amount of fishing in very difficult pockets. Pockets are never very easy matters for either schoolboys or schoolgirls to get to the bottom of, and certainly Maggie's contained an extraordinary jumble of treasures. At last out came—not the letter, but a string of white beads, that fell on the pavement with a very decided rattle. Notwithstanding books and slates, however, they had hardly touched the ground before Maggie had seized them; but quick as she was, Minnie had already espied them.

"What is it, Maggie?" she asked.

"Nothing," said Maggie, slipping them into her pocket.

"Oh, Maggie, what nonsense! Do let me see, it looked like a bracelet."

"It was not, indeed, it was only a string of beads."

"I know," said her companion, looking very wise. "It was your rosary."

"Well, and if it was, what then?" inquired Maggie, not the very picture of a Christian.

"Why, nothing; but you need not look so vexed. I wish you would show it to me, I never saw one in my life."

"Just to let you make fun of it, I suppose, as you all did of everything you had ever heard of in our religion, the other day."

"I am sure, Maggie, I said very little; I only said I shouldn't like to have to tell all my sins to a priest. Do show it to me."

There was so much sweetness in the face and tone of the little pleader, that, dragon as she was in defending her religion against the taunts of her schoolfellows, Maggie could not refuse, and, after a little more difficult fishing, she laid the white beads in her companion's hand.

"What a pretty little thing!" cried Minnie, in admiration. "Are these chains silver?"

"Yes, and so is the cross. It was mamma's present the day of my—"

"Of your what, Maggie? Do tell me."

"Of my first communion."

"Oh, I see," said Minnie, looking very grave; "have you been confirmed?"

"Yes, some time since."

"I am to be confirmed the summer after next, I think," said Minnie.

"When did you make your first communion?" asked her friend.

"We haven't such a thing in our church?" replied Minnie, unconsciously speaking the truth; "that is, I mean," she added, correcting herself, "not as you have, to be dressed all in white for it. I suppose I shall receive the sacrament sometimes, when I am grown up; but I don't know, mamma never 'stops,' neither does papa."

Maggie was too polite to look horrified, so she swallowed her astonishment, and remained silent.

"I wish you would tell me what you do with this," said Minnie, who had returned to the examination of the rosary.

"What would be the use?—you would not understand me if I did."

"Why not?" asked Minnie, looking as if a slight had been passed upon her powers of comprehension.

"Well, I say my prayers with it."

"I know that, but how? Why are these five beads larger than the others?"

"Because we say Our Fathers to them, and Hail Marys to the little ones."

"I have often heard people speak of the Hail Mary. Is it a long prayer?"

"No, very short. Listen: 'Hail Mary, full of grace, the Lord is with thee, blessed art thou amongst women, and blessed is the fruit of thy womb, Jesus. Holy Mary, Mother of God, pray for us sinners, now, and at the hour of our death. Amen.' There, now, I suppose, Minnie, you are quite shocked."

"No, I am not, though of course it doesn't seem right to me to say prayers to any one but God."

"And yet half the Hail Mary is taken out of the Bible," said Maggie. "It ought to be a good prayer, for it took the holy angel Gabriel, St. Elizabeth, and the Church to make it; and it is a good prayer too," she added, warmly, "it gets me everything I want, if I ought to have it."

Minnie opened her eyes.

"It does, indeed," continued Maggie. "Whenever I am in any little trouble, or am anxious about anything, I say a Hail Mary, and everything seems to go right directly."

"But why don't you ask God Himself straight off?"

"Why did you ask Miss Edwards to get your lesson excused the other afternoon, instead of going 'straight off' to Mrs. Brown yourself? Miss Edwards has no power to excuse lessons."

"No, I know that, but then I knew she would ask for me so much better than I could for myself, and could tell Mrs. Brown just how difficult I found it to learn; and, besides, Mrs. Brown is so fond of her that she never refuses her anything."

"Then, Minnie, you yourself have explained why we pray to our Blessed Lady first, as well as Father O'Brien ever did in a sermon! Fancy how well the Mother of God can ask things of her Son, and how dearly Almighty God loves her. Why, the difference between our prayer and hers would be the difference between the strumming of a child on the old school piano and the music of a hundred glorious church organs playing all together!"

Minnie felt very uncertain as to the amount

of harmony such a concert would produce, but she understood what Maggie wished her to understand, and felt the truth of it. She, however, made no remark, but only took another look at the rosary.

"If you like I will explain it to you altogether," said Maggie, who began to be considerably softened by the almost reverential manner of her little companion.

"Do," said Minnie, eagerly. "Do you know, Maggie, ever since you came to our school I have wondered at so many things about your religion, though I have never liked to ask you any questions? You are the only Catholic I ever saw, or even heard of, except in histories of England. I suppose you would not come to Mrs. Brown's if there were a Catholic school near."

"No, that I certainly should not. But Mrs. Brown is very good; she is always very careful to send me away to practise during the Bible classes, and never lets me do any of your historical lessons. I read history to mamma at home instead."

"Now tell me about the rosary," said Minnie.

"Well, it is divided into five joyful, five sorrowful, and five glorious mysteries. Each of these mysteries has something to do with our Lord's life or passion, and we think of this, whatever it may be, while we say the Our Father, ten Hail Marys, and the Glory be to the Father, at the end. If you look at my rosary, you will see it is divided into five parts, which we call decades, and, according to the day of the week, we say either the joyful, sorrowful, or glorious mysteries. Suppose it were Monday or Thursday, while I said the prayers of the first decade I should think of the Annunciation. I should fancy our Blessed Lady kneeling in her own quiet little room, and suddenly the angel appearing before her, all light and glory, and telling her that she should be the mother of the Redeemer that all the world had been looking for since the days of Adam."

"But, Maggie—"

"What, dear?"

"How could you be thinking of one thing and saying another all the time?"

"Very easily; even in things of the world we often say words, under certain circumstances, that would have quite a different meaning and effect under others. If I say the prayers while I am thinking of the joyful mysteries, I have a kind of happy feeling about me as I meditate on the holy joy that each of them caused our Blessed Mother. This makes me think of everything that I myself have reason to feel joyful about too. I think of the goodness of God, of the love our Lord has for us, of the prayers of the Blessed Virgin, and of all the bright and happy things that God has showered down upon the world, and somehow it seems all woven together with the Hail Marys into one joyful prayer. But when I think of the sorrowful mysteries, it is quite different. I say, 'Holy Mary, Mother of God, pray for us sinners,' with very penitent thoughts, when I see every drop of the blood of Jesus trickling down upon the ground for my sins! Listen, Minnie, I think I can make you understand this. Supposing, after a young lady had been married about a month, her greatest friend went to see her for the first time since her marriage. Can you fancy her going into the nice new house, bright and pretty as brides' homes always are? Perhaps her first words might be, 'Mary, I have thought of you so much during the last few weeks.' What kind, happy, joyous words they would be, while her mind was full of her friend's happiness, with her kind husband and happy home. Well, then, suppose that six months afterwards the gentleman was killed by falling from his horse, and that the lady was so far from home at the time that she did not see her widowed friend for some weeks. Suppose, as she went into the same room, her first words were the same as those she had spoken before, what mournful, grieving, agonising words they would be while her mind was full of the dead husband and the great sorrow of her friend. Do you see what I mean? The mystery casts, as it were, a shadow over the prayer, so that, though we use the same words over and over again, they seem to have a fresh meaning every time. Can you not see how this is?"

"Yes, quite well; now tell us what the other mysteries are."

"In the second joyful mystery we think of the Blessed Virgin, instead of being proud of her great dignity, going out to see and wait upon her old relation St. Elizabeth. But the third is my favourite of all the joyful mysteries, for it is the birth of our dear Lord in the grotto at Bethlehem, and if I love Him more in one way than another, it is when I think of Him as a little tiny baby. I feel sometimes as if I could never leave this decade, even to go on with the others. Then comes the presentation in the Temple, with Anna and old Simeon standing by; and lastly we have the finding of our Lord in the Temple, after His Blessed Mother and St. Joseph had been searching for Him everywhere for three days."

"These are very nice to think about," said Minnie, gently; "I almost feel as if I should like to say the rosary myself."

Maggie smiled. "Next come the five sorrowful mysteries, and we say them on Tuesday and Friday. In the first we see Jesus lying on the ground in the cold dark night, in the garden of Olives. Do you know, Minnie, that as He laid there He saw every single sin of every single man who will ever have lived, and His sorrow was so great as He looked at them, that His heart overflowed, and forced the blood through His very flesh! But the next mystery is sadder still, for it is the scourging of our Lord by the cruel Roman soldiers. Papa says, if He had not been God, He must have died under the torture; but He made Himself live that He might suffer more. Next comes the crowning with thorns, then the carrying of the hard heavy cross up the steep hill of Calvary, with the people shrieking and hooting after Him, and driving Him on, though He was fainting from weariness. Last of all, in the fifth mystery, we see Him dying for our sins."

"Maggie," cried the little listener, whose large blue eyes were full of tears, "these are very, very beautiful, but tell me the glorious mysteries."

"The Resurrection, the Ascension, the Descent of the Holy Ghost, the Assumption, and the Coronation; we say them on Wednesdays and Saturdays."

"What do you mean by the 'Assumption' and 'Coronation'?"

"They are the very two mysteries that give us so much confidence in the intercession of our Blessed Lady, for we believe that after she was dead, God took her soul and body up to heaven, and crowned her queen of both men and angels. But leaving out these two, which of course you do not understand, is not the rosary beautiful?"

"Very beautiful, I cannot tell you how much I like it. But even now, Maggie—don't be vexed—I wish the prayers were to God instead of Hail Marys."

"Because you are a Protestant, dear. Perhaps some day our dear Lord will teach you how much we love and honour Him by loving and honouring His Blessed Mother for His sake. I shall pray very hard for you, for you would make such a dear little Catholic! Good-bye."

Maggie was such an earnest, pious little girl, that I am sure she kept her word; perhaps, too, Minnie prayed for herself. However this may be, certain it is, that there is a sweet little Sister of Charity whose name in the world was Minnie, and who of all beautiful devotions loves her rosary best. She said it in sorrow long ago, when her conversion seemed a thing that would never be forgiven; and later still, when her vocation seemed a thing that could never be followed; and her Catholic Father now blesses his child, and she has worn the white cornette for many a long day. She has said it in joy by the happy deathbeds of sinners it had seemed impossible to convert, and over the return of prodigal men and women it had seemed impossible to reclaim. And once a year she says it three times round, for a certain Maggie who is now the mother of half a dozen sturdy boys, and that on the anniversary of a day when two little girls had a quiet chat in the quiet street of the quiet little town of N.

THE WHITE ANGEL.

CHAPTER I.

IT was a sultry afternoon, so sultry that the very trees stood still in their laziness; the little birds hardly twittered in their nests; while puss, forgetting there was such a thing as a mouse in the world, was stretched full length in the marjoram. But the bustle in the schoolroom went on just the same as usual, and the pianos jingled just as fast as though the little people had no time to be warm, nor their little fingers time to feel tired.

Mrs. Glover's was a very busy house. From that lady herself, always gliding from room to room, and from one class to another, down to little tiny Eva, nobody ever wasted a minute all the day long. Teachers, children, servants, all were busy, and there was not an idle thing belonging to the house except the old grey cat I just told you about, who was rolling over and over among the herbs. Perhaps, however, my little reader is beginning to think, "If these little girls were always so busy, they could not have had much time for play." I only wish you could have seen them at their recreation! What games they had! What romps! What fun! With their long ropes and skipping ropes, their battledores and shuttlecocks, their old games and new games, and the large green swing at the end of the playground! I do not believe there ever was such a pretty house, such a large shady playground, nor such happy, joyous little girls anywhere else in the world as there used to be at Mrs. Glover's school. Shall I tell you what it was like?

It was a large white house, with clean-looking green Venetian shutters, and such a lovely garden, so full of roses and lilies, pinks and stocks, that everybody who went by used to peep over the hedge and long for a nosegay. Mrs. Glover was very kind, though, like every other really kind schoolmistress, she was also very strict. And yet there were persons who thought her strictness rather peculiar. Although she considered a badly learned lesson or carelessly written copy as a waste of time, she would often make an excuse for a little girl's negligence that the child herself had in no way expected; but with real faults of character the case was very different. A falsehood, an act of disobedience, or a fit of sullenness, was, she would say, an offence against God. This she never excused; so that to be really naughty at Harford House was the sure way to get into disgrace. To the credit of the pupils, however, I must say that punishments were very rare, and when they were inflicted, however sad the little offender might feel, I am quite sure good, kind Mrs. Glover felt sadder still.

The second class had been sitting very still under the care of Miss Moreland, the English teacher, all this warm afternoon. The windows were open and the blinds drawn down, but though the sun was shut out, the heat contrived to steal in, and made a great many curly heads feel very tired and warm. Never had little folks felt less inclined for hard work. It was a great deal too hot to skip over seas and oceans, and from one continent to another, and never had places been so hard to find, and outlandish names so difficult to pronounce. Suddenly the door opened and Mrs. Glover appeared.

"I have just given my class permission, my dear Miss Moreland," she remarked, "to leave off their lessons, and to take their work into the dining-room, which is the only cool room in the house. Can you arrange for your little ladies to join us?"

Miss Moreland's smile was answer sufficient, and a general move was made to clear the books and slates—not a very long business when an afternoon with Mrs. Glover was in prospect.

"Please do not be vexed, Miss Moreland," said Emily Weston, a little girl about twelve years of age, "but I really think I must have dropped my thimble in the playground before dinner, for I cannot find it anywhere."

"That was very careless, Emily; you had better go and see. You are generally pretty careful, so I am not vexed, though you must, of course, forfeit your 'order mark' for to-day."

Emily sighed, and walked off to the playground to look for her missing thimble. And a fine hunt she had! First all over the playground, then in the schoolroom, then again in the playground. Never was anything so provoking, never was weather so warm, and, to tell the truth, never, perhaps, was Emily so cross. At last, after about ten minutes' search, there was the thimble on one of the benches, looking just as cool and matter-of-fact as though it had all the right in the world to be there and nowhere else.

"Aggravating little thing!" cried Emily, seizing it crossly. "I have lost my order mark, and been kept for full ten minutes out of the dining-room, where I might have been so happy, and all through you."

"All through you," thought the thimble, and only wished he could say so.

Emily turned towards the house, and had just entered the broad walk leading to it, when the sound of a drum caught her attention. It came evidently enough from the street before the house, and was beaten so vigorously that the little girl's heart went pit-a-pat with excitement. What could it be? What an unusual sound in the little town of Enbury! And such a buzz and shouting of children! She stood still to listen. "What would I give to be at our dormitory window!" she thought. "I should be able to see what it was then. I have a good mind to run up, I wouldn't stop a minute—but then it is forbidden. There could not surely be any harm in it, though, and nobody will ever know."

"But you have wasted more than ten minutes already," whispered Conscience, "and this is not recreation time."

"And as two minutes more will make no difference," pleaded Emily, in answer to the little monitor, "Mrs. Glover will not be more vexed with me for wasting twelve minutes than she would have been for ten, and I shall have had the satisfaction of knowing what the drum is beating for. There it is again. I will go."

"Disobedience," said Conscience.

"I don't care," cried Emily, "it is the first drum I ever heard, and I must know what is the matter," and before Conscience had time to speak again, the little girl was at the dormitory window, peeping over the muslin blind.

To Emily's vexation, however, the solution of the mystery was still a long way off, for the drum, although so loud, was in reality at a considerable distance from the house, and the thick trees that were before it concealed everything from its windows, except that part of the street just in front of the gates. But she kept her place, for the sound was evidently approaching, as it grew louder every moment, mingled with a strange kind of instrument, and the repetition of something every now and then in a nasal twang, most wonderful to hear. Whatever could it be? The happy afternoon with Mrs. Glover and the broken rule were both forgotten in the intensity of her curiosity. At last it came near, shadows flitted among the trees, a group of children filled the road in front, staring behind them at something slowly following. It came in sight— a little dog with a paper frill, a thin, pale woman carrying a bundle, and, last of all, a shabby man with a drum and pipes, bearing on his back the brilliantly painted framework of a "Punch and Judy"

The White Angel. 21

There was a halt, the man and woman held a little conference, and then the drum commenced a new succession of flourishes, Pan's pipes set off in accompaniment, and in a few minutes Punch, Judy, the baby, and Toby were squealing, squeaking, barking, and fighting to perfection. Emily was enchanted, never had the little girl seen anything half so interesting. Not to be obliged, however, to stand quite so much on tiptoe, she tried to pull the blind a little lower, and had just succeeded when snap went the string. In a terrible fright she tried to readjust it, but in vain, for the tape, broken in the middle, only pulled out farther at every attempt. The performance came to an end, the showman emerged from his box, while his wife went round collecting the pence and halfpence of the company, and chancing to glance up at the now uncurtained window, discovered Emily. Poor child! Hers was not an enviable situation, with the hot sun streaming full upon her, the broken blind within, and the importunate woman without, and she without a copper to satisfy her. To break a rule of the school was to forfeit the weekly half-holiday, and how could she escape detection unless she could arrange the blind again? If anybody should chance to see that woman, too, it would be all over with her. But there she stood, although Emily shook her head till you might have taken her for a little Chinese mandarin, for she thought (and not unnaturally) that if the poor folks could give their halfpence, the young lady at the big house should not refuse hers. Emily grew desperate, she thrust her hand in her pocket, to see if a stray penny could possibly be lurking in one of the corners; but no, not one. She took out her purse. There lay the half-crown aunty had given her, and a shilling, nothing else. At this instant she thought she heard a step on the stairs, and opening the window with a sudden jerk, she threw the shilling into the plate, and pulling down the holland blind to hide the dilapidation, slipped behind the door. But before the blind had descended, a look of gratitude such as one seldom sees, shot from the poor woman's eyes. "God bless you," she cried, "God bless you!" but the blessing did not fall on the little girl, for there had been no charity in her gift.

Nobody came, for the footfall had only existed in Emily's fancy, and she stole out of her hiding-place. "I must run the risk of being seen, and stop and mend the curtain properly with fresh tape," was the conclusion she came to. She felt very miserable, for all the excitement she had had in Punch and Judy had passed, and she began to wonder how she could ever have cared for anything so silly. She had hidden like a thief, she now crept down-stairs like one; if anybody should meet her! Only fancy! She ransacked her workbox, but no tape was to be found. She looked at the clock and found that a full half-hour had passed since the girls had left the schoolroom, and she had asked Miss Moreland for two or three minutes, and yet, come what would, the string must be mended. At this moment a workbox on a very tidy shelf caught her eye.

"Dear Katie," she cried, "I am sure she would let me have a piece of her tape if she knew how much I wanted it, for she is the kindest friend I have, although she is the eldest girl in the school. I wonder what she would think if she knew what I had been doing, for they say she never broke a rule in her life. But then she is a saint, and I don't profess to be so good as she is. I must take care she never does know it. How I wish I had gone into the dining-room as soon as I had found my thimble!"

Emily soon found all that she wanted in Katie Dawson's box, and again gliding up-stairs, after what seemed to her an age, the blind was mended, and once again restored to its place.

"Let me see, was the window open or shut?" pondered Emily. "Why, shut to be sure, because I had to open it for the woman. Oh, my poor shilling!"

It was in vain, however, that Emily tried to shut the window, pushing it first up and then down with a jar that it frightened her to hear. To a certain point it went very well, but beyond that, yield it would not, and she was obliged to give it up in despair; so pulling down the holland blind once more, and thrusting the broken tapes in her pocket, she went down-stairs.

By the time Emily entered the dining-room another ten minutes had elapsed. Mrs. Glover was reading a tale in which Emily had been deeply interested, and of which they had just reached the prettiest part. That lady paused as she entered, and looked at her in astonishment.

"Why, Emily! Where have you been all this time, for it seems, by your box in your hand, that this is your first appearance? What have you been doing?"

". Miss Moreland gave me permission to look for my thimble," replied Emily, blushing deeply.

"Yes, but not to spend nearly three-quarters of an hour doing so," said Miss Moreland, looking at her watch; "you have not surely been all this time looking for that, my dear?"

Emily hung down her head, she did not attempt a reply.

The White Angel.

"No, I see how it is," replied Mrs. Glover, "you have been amusing yourself. Well, since you have chosen to commence your recreation in this manner, you will finish it in the same way. Go into the schoolroom now and do whatever you choose, you will study during the recreation time to-morrow morning instead!"

Poor Emily! As she left the room with thirty pairs of eyes full upon her, I do not think any of my little readers would have changed places with her for a much greater pleasure than to see a "Punch and Judy."

CHAPTER II.

"IF you please, Miss Moreland, the carrier has brought a parcel for Miss Dawson," said an old servant entering the room just as tea was over; "and he says there's a shilling to pay."

Katie took out her purse. "He must give me change, then, for half-a-crown," she observed, handing it to Simpson, who left the room, but almost immediately returned. "He says he has no change, miss."

"What must we do?" asked Katie; "will any one lend me a shilling?"

Nearly every one was by this time in the garden, and of the few girls who lingered, waiting for Katie, not one had the sum required.

"I beg your pardon, Miss Weston," said Simpson to Emily, who was hurrying away without appearing to hear Katie's question, "but I think, if I remember, I gave you a shilling change out of the wool last night. I'm pretty sure I did; maybe you'll be so good as to lend it to Miss Dawson."

Emily crimsoned to the temples. Hers was naturally a candid disposition, and quite unpractised at deceit.

"Did you, Simpson? I will look and see," and she began fumbling in her pocket.

"Emily," cried Katie, misconstruing her look, "I can see you do not wish to lend me the money, and it does not matter, the carrier can call again to-morrow. I shall have change by then." She spoke quietly, but Emily saw that she was surprised and hurt at what she considered her unwillingness to oblige her.

"Really, really, Katie, it is not that, but this is all I have," and she held up her sole remaining coin.

"Then, my dear," said the old servant, kindly, "you certainly must have lost a shilling, for you have been nowhere to spend it, and I am certain I gave you one last night. You remember it, do you not?"

"Yes," said Emily, faintly.

"Well, then, we had better have a look for

it, for shillings are shillings, and don't drop out of the clouds. I'll ask Mrs. Glover to pay for this, Miss Katie."

"Very well, do."

"Emily dear," she exclaimed, as soon as Simpson had left the room, "what is the matter, you look so strange?"

"Nothing," said Emily, pettishly, and shaking off the arm Katie had thrown fondly round her.

"Why, Emmy, this is not like you," cried her companion, more and more astonished. "I daresay you are vexed about your shilling, but I will help you to look for it."

"No, thank you, I don't care about it a bit. I wish you would leave me alone."

"Certainly, if I only vex you, it is not worth while my staying, for they are waiting for me in the garden." She left the room as she spoke with tears in her eyes.

"O dear, O dear!" exclaimed Emily, "that dreadful, dreadful Punch and Judy! Another misery! Now I have offended the dearest, kindest friend I have in all the school. How cross I was to her! How I wish I dared tell her. But if I did, she would never like me again, nor take any more notice of me;" and feeling quite disinclined for play, the little girl took her seat on a low form, and began to unrol her needlework.

The door opened, and Simpson entered to clear the tea-table.

"Well, Miss Weston, have you found your shilling?"

"No," said Emily, "but it is of no consequence, it doesn't matter."

"But it does matter, Mrs. Glover would be very vexed if she knew."

So thought Emily, and almost jumped off the form in her fright.

"Perhaps you dropped it," said Simpson, too intent on packing the cups and saucers to notice Emily's start.

"No, I did not, I know."

"Well, then," said Simpson, "all I know is that things can't go without hands, and as I said just now, shillings are shillings."

Emily knew that very well, but she also knew to her cost that secrets are secrets.

The table was cleared, the tray piled up ready to be carried away, and yet Simpson lingered.

"Miss Weston," she began, walking up to her, and speaking in a low mysterious tone.

Emily looked up.

"Did you leave your purse in that frock pocket this morning?"

"Yes, I always do."

"Well, then," said Simpson, sinking her voice

still lower, "I have my suspicions. Your shilling is not the only thing that has been lost lately. I have my suspicions about somebody, though I won't say who; but I caught that very somebody sneaking about in the dressing room where the afternoon dresses hang, only this very morning. It doesn't do for us to judge, I know, but depend upon it, Miss Emily, that 'somebody' has got your shilling."

"No, no," cried Emily, in an agony, "pray, Simpson, don't say such a wicked thing as that. I would rather lose a hundred shillings than think any such thing!"

"I am not in the habit of saying 'wicked things' that I know of, Miss Weston," cried Simpson, drawing herself up, "but people must use the eyes and senses that God has given them, or what have they got them for?"

"But, Simpson, listen," exclaimed Emily, half beside herself with the idea that an innocent person should be blamed on her account, "I don't care about the shilling at all. Please do not say a word about this to Mrs. Glover, for I am certain you are mistaken."

"Well, I only hope I am, but you know, Miss Weston, to hold one's tongue is not always to do justice to other folks. I must say I always feel uncomfortable when I see things go like this."

"But promise me that you will not say anything about it to any one else."

"Well, it's no business of mine, I suppose," answered the old woman, taking up the tray, and with this indefinite reply to her request poor Emily was obliged to rest satisfied.

An hour of the bright summer evening passed and found her still stitching away on her low form in the corner, and brooding over her troubles, when a sunny little figure suddenly bounded in from the garden.

"Any girls here?" Yes, you, Emmy. Come along, such fun! We are all in the flower-garden, Mrs. Glover and all; don't stop, or you'll be too late;" and without another word Eva was off like a lapwing, her bright curls streaming far away behind her. Emily followed. Ordinarily the flower-garden was forbidden ground, but now its pretty lawn was crowded with girls, while Mrs. Glover and the teachers were seated on a green bench at the head of it.

"Whatever can they be doing?" speculated Emily, as she reached the garden gate.

"Come, my dear child," said Miss Moreland, turning her head at the rattling of the latch, "just in time."

The farther end of the lawn was not visible from the gate, and Emily advanced, still puzzled as to the cause of so much animation, and had nearly reached her governess when Punch's squeak burst upon her ear. She started and coloured in an instant.

"Silly child," said Mrs. Glover, holding out her hand; "it is only a puppet-show. Doctor Evans saw them standing before the window, and sent them up to play for you. He thought you would be amused, and I daresay you will. Did you ever see one before?"

"Yes," said Emily, turning away her face.

"Not in Enbury though, I think," observed Miss Moreland. "I was just remarking to Mrs Glover that this is the first time I ever met with one in this part of the country."

Had Emily's answer been ever so lucid, it would have been unheard amid the vigorous concert now commencing, and catching sight of Katie, at this moment looking towards her, she joined her on the grass.

Although in her ill-temper Emily had voted Punch stupid, and a silly thing, no one enjoyed his vagaries more than she, now that she could do so without a twinge of conscience. When the performance was over, and the showman arranging his puppets, Eva was despatched to the house for some bones for poor Toby. The woman walked towards Mrs. Glover, who took out her purse.

"The gentleman has paid me already, ma'am,

and very well too. God bless him! Ah, lady, but ours is a hard life!"

"So I suppose."

"It is indeed; we've done well to-day, but we don't often get such luck, I can tell you. And it's not before we wanted it, for we've left two children down at the bottom of the town, almost walked off their legs, poor things."

"They look very poor," whispered Katie; "please, Mrs. Glover, may we make a subscription for them?"

"If you like, but mind, as they are strangers, I restrict it to a penny each."

"In a few minutes the little plate was piled high with pence, and as it was handed to the showman's wife, it would be hard to say whether she or her kind little friends looked the brighter. Even Emily forgot her discomfiture as she placed a borrowed penny on the plate. She was standing by Mrs. Glover, when, Punch and his train being ready to depart, the woman again approached to bid that lady good evening.

"Good evening," said Mrs. Glover, with a kind smile; "I wish you success."

"Thank you kindly, ma'am; as for you, miss," added the woman as she passed Emily, "God will reward you."

The White Angel.

"Why, what has this young lady done for you?" asked Mrs. Glover, much surprised.

"She gave me a whole shilling, ma'am, and that's something for a little miss like her. The Lord bless her! Good night, ma'am."

Emily's face was crimson in the intensity of her agitation.

"My dear child," said Mrs. Glover, "though there is a great merit in keeping our good deeds secret, there is no occasion to blush about them like that. And so you gave the poor woman a shilling! Well, it was an act of charity, and performed with a pure intention, or you would not look so pained at your secret being discovered. But another time, my child, I should like you to consult Miss Moreland or myself before giving away so much. I suppose your gift was made before my restriction."

"Yes," replied Emily, hardly knowing what she said.

"I need not have asked, for I know very well that disobedience is not one of your faults."

Poor Emily!

"There now, run and play with the others," said Mrs. Glover, stroking her hair. "Stop a minute, though," she added, laughing, "how long have you indulged in a train? What is that hanging down?"

D

It was the broken string, which she had forgotten to take out of her pocket.

"It is a piece of tape I meant to have put in my box," said Emily, in desperation.

Imagine, my little reader, how you, or any other candid little girl, would have felt at being praised as Mrs. Glover praised Emily, if, like her, you had deserved punishment instead. Bitter indeed she began to find the fruit of her disobedience, like those apples the old writers tell us of, growing on the shores of the Dead Sea, which, bright and pleasant to the eye, crumbled to nauseous ashes in the mouth. As, gathering the string up hastily into her pocket, she once more disappeared among the girls, she longed to turn back to her kind governess and confess the whole, but she could not do this. Emily Weston was clever, amiable, and good-natured, but she had no moral courage. She had never, perhaps, in her life told a direct falsehood, but she had not always firmness to declare the truth, and was therefore sometimes led into equivocation, which we all know is nearly as bad, and it may be in some cases even worse than a direct lie.

"And so you found your shilling after all?" whispered Katie, as they were kneeling side by side waiting for Mrs. Glover to come in to say the night prayers with them.

"What do you mean?" asked Emily, who began to think that the shilling had a ghost that was never to be laid.

"I know all about it. Eva has told me that you gave it to the woman to-night. You are a dear good child, Emmy. I was very unkind to feel so cross with you. Where did you find it?" At this moment Mrs. Glover entered, and the prayers commenced.

It was Emily's week to answer, but her voice faltered so much that, thinking her unwell, Mrs. Glover directed Katie to take her place. Poor Emily had many distractions. How could she examine her conscience with any contrition for her sins, when her very last act, even upon her knees, had been a tacit deceit she had no intention of repairing. One sin always leads to another, and Emily said no night prayers at all. When they rose from their knees she did not venture another look at Katie, but, thankful that their beds were at opposite ends of the dormitory, walked slowly, sadly, and silently up-stairs.

For nearly two hours Emily lay tossing and turning, first on one side and then on the other. Had she not enough to keep her awake in the sad recollections of this unfortunate day? She slept at last, but towards morning was again aroused by a commotion in the bedroom.

"What is the matter?" she asked, raising herself upon her elbow.

"Dear me, Emily! How soundly you must sleep! Don't you hear the storm?" asked one of the girls.

"The worst of it is," cried another, "that the window next Katie's bed has been left open, and nobody can shut it. Hark at the blind flapping up and down! It is quite wet through already, for the wind sets this way."

"The question is," exclaimed Miss Moreland, "who can have opened it? This window has not been raised at the bottom all the half-year, because, though easy enough to push up, it is next to impossible to shut it. Simpson and Mary tried for half an hour the last time it was opened, and were obliged to fetch the gardener in after all. He said it wanted repairing in some way."

Emily laid herself down to brood over this fresh discomfiture, and meantime the rain came in faster than ever.

"Call Mrs. Glover," said one of the girls.

"No, don't!" cried Emily, starting up.

"It is all very well for you, Emily, who are at the other end of the room, but how would you like to sleep in that bed yourself? Will you change places with Katie?"

"Yes, I will," cried Emily, springing out of bed.

"Nonsense, silly child," exclaimed Miss Moreland, "go back to your place. We shall have Mrs. Glover in without sending for her, if you make so much noise, young ladies. No, the only thing to be done is for Katie to take refuge with the owner of the largest bed, and we will pin the sheets of hers up to the window." And the best arrangement having been made that this uncomfortable position would allow, all were soon asleep again but Emily.

CHAPTER III.

THE next morning was so wet and gloomy, although the storm had ceased, that the girls were obliged to take their recreation in the large schoolroom, instead of going into the playground. It was a relief to Emily that as yet the question of the window had been only discussed among themselves, a severe headache having detained Mrs. Glover in her room much later than usual.

"You remember, I presume, Emily, that your recreation time is forfeited this morning?"

"Yes, Miss Moreland, I am getting my books."

"You had better take them into the little class-room, as we are going to be here."

Emily obeyed, but as the rooms were connected she could hear everything that passed among the girls.

"What are you looking for, Katie?" asked one of them, after they had been sitting working and chatting for nearly half an hour.

"Do you remember that Father Gilbert gave Mrs. Glover the measure of the high altar the other day?"

"Yes, what about it?"

"Mrs. Glover gave it to me to keep for her, and somebody has been to my box and cut more than half of it off."

"Who could have done it?" asked Miss Moreland.

"Somebody who wanted a piece of tape, I suppose."

"Very rude of somebody, then," said Miss Moreland.

"Oh, no," cried Katie, "they knew they would have been welcome to anything of mine, and of course had no idea of what mischief they were doing. What will Father Gilbert think, and whatever will Mrs. Glover say?"

"Here she comes," said Miss Moreland, and Emily heard the rustle of her dress.

"Good morning, young ladies," she began, and Emily could tell by her tone how severe she looked. "I have a very serious question to ask, and I beg of you in your answer to tell

The White Angel.

me 'the truth, the whole truth, and nothing but the truth.' You were some of you disturbed in the night, I find, by one of the bedroom windows having been left open. Now, I have questioned every servant in the house, and they all assure me that it was not opened by any of them. Mary tells me that she closed the windows and pulled down the blinds at four o'clock, as I desire her to do every day this warm weather, as the sun is then full on the windows. If, then, they speak the truth, the window must have been opened by one of the young ladies. I therefore ask whether any of you did so or not."

There was no reply.

"I am of course aware," continued Mrs. Glover, "that to have done so you must have broken a rule; but I trust that no fear of punishment would deter any of you from acknowledging the truth boldly. I therefore ask you once again, young ladies, did any of you open the window?"

Again there was a dead silence.

"In justice to each one of you, and to the servants, I must put you even yet to a severe test. Miss Dawson, did you open the window?"

"Indeed I did not," answered Katie's clear, ringing voice, and the same answer fell, as though stereotyped, from thirty voices in succession.

"Then, now," said Mrs. Glover, and Emily heard her rise from her seat—"now I am convinced that one of the servants must have told me an untruth, and I must act accordingly. No one who can descend to a falsehood must remain in my house."

Strange that nobody thought of the *absent* pupil. What should she do, sit still and hear another charged as a liar for her fault? Was not this tacitly bearing "false witness against her neighbour"? As speculation after speculation as to who the offender could be, fell on her ear from the adjoining room, she felt, if possible, more than miserable.

Although the truth was not for an instant suspected, Emily's troubles did not end here. Towards evening Katie was seized with a severe face-ache, which, patiently as she bore.it, was almost too much for her fortitude.

"How do you think you could have caught it, my poor child?" asked Miss Moreland, as she sat pale and faint with the pain.

"Really, Miss Moreland, I am afraid it was from the window last night. I did not like to disturb you at first, so I bore the draught for some time, until I began to fear it would make me really ill. But I shall be better soon, I daresay," she added, with one of her own sweet smiles.

"I hope you will, indeed, for you would not enjoy tea at the farm half so much if you had the tooth-ache, would you, Katie?" asked little Eva. "I will say a whole rosary for you to get well."

"Thank you," said Katie, kissing her, "you are very good to me, Eva."

"So I ought to be, because you are good to everybody, and because you are my little mother. Katie, when I am a big girl like you I shall try and be as good as you are."

"And a great deal better, I hope," whispered Katie.

Thursday morning dawned bright and beautiful after the rain, but not one whit brighter than the joyous faces that welcomed it, all gay in anticipation of the promised treat. But the sunshine of to-day was as gloomy to Emily as the clouds of yesterday, for how could she rejoice among good and happy children, or look forward with pleasure to a treat in which she had not the shadow of a right to participate? Besides, Katie's face was not better, and Emily felt only too truly that she was the cause of all the pain her friend was suffering.

As usual after breakfast, the children spread themselves over the playground, but Emily had no heart to join them, and wandered away from the noisy party into a little shrubbery at the extreme end of the garden. It was not very extensive, but small as it was, it contained a pretty little chapel dedicated to the Blessed Virgin, which the devotion of the children kept always adorned with their own needlework, and bright and fragrant with flowers, and to which they would often steal away in the midst of their games, to say a decade of the rosary, or to pray for a companion's intention. A little figure was already kneeling before the altar as Emily entered the chapel—it was Eva.

Emily knelt beside her and kissed her. "What are you doing here, Eva?"

"I am just going to say the rosary to ask our Blessed Lady to make Katie better, her face is so bad."

"I wish you would say one to make me better."

"But you are not ill, are you?" asked Eva, opening her blue eyes very wide.

"Yes, I am—ill—wretched—wrong altogether!"

"Poor Emily! well, which is the worst, you or Katie?"

"I am, but in a different way."

"What is the matter with you?"

"Everything. I am very miserable, Eva, very miserable indeed;" and hiding her face in her hands, Emily burst into a passionate flood of tears.

The White Angel. 43

"Poor dear Emmy," cried the sympathising little girl, getting up and twining her arms round the neck of her kneeling companion—"poor dear Emmy, I am so sorry for you."

"What do you do when you are naughty, Eva?" asked Emily, after a short pause.

"I don't know," said Eva, looking rather ashamed; "cry and stamp sometimes, I think."

"Yes, but I don't mean then, I mean afterwards, when you are sorry and want to be good."

"I come here and ask our Blessed Lady to help me, and somehow she always does."

"Will you ask her just the same thing for me, Eva?"

"But you are not naughty, you have not been crying and stamping. You are as good as— well, *almost* as good as Katie."

"Oh, Eva, if you only knew!"

Eva said no more, but resuming her place commenced her rosary. Emily watched her as she knelt, her earnest eyes fixed on the pure white image above, but her baby heart far away at the feet of the Mother it symbolised. Sweet little Eva! the white beads did their work. As Emily thought calmly over the events of the last two days, of the broken rule, the suspected theft, the undeserved praise, the disobedience unacknowledged by her, imputed as a lie to another, and of poor Katie's indisposition, caused by her indiscretion,—as all these things passed through her mind, she realised for the first time how much she must have offended God. Tiny Eva did not know how sincere an act of contrition was rising beside her; her eyes were too much engrossed to see even one tear fall on the altar steps, but the angels of heaven saw it, and rejoiced, and the Queen of the angels saw it from her starry throne, and how she loved the little penitent! Then came a thought into Emily's mind, only sad at first, until another glance at the wrong she had done made her rejoice even in its sadness. Do you ask, little reader, what this was? Emily had broken the rule—Emily's thought was to bear the punishment. At first she shrank from Mrs. Glover's anger, the loss of the pleasure party, the surprise of her schoolfellows, and Katie's sorrow; but she only bowed her head the lower, and before Eva rose from her knees, Emily was standing before her governess.

And she told her all without remark, without suppression, to the smallest particle of her tale. As Mrs. Glover had said the day before, she spoke "the truth, the whole truth, and nothing but the truth." Then came a long silence. Emily knew that Mrs. Glover was strict, and trembled with downcast eyes.

"Emily," said the low voice of her governess.

She glanced up; the kind face beside her was bright with one of its sweetest smiles.

"Emily, my child," said Mrs. Glover, "I congratulate you—yes, congratulate you—for the battle was hard to fight, the victory hard to win, and yet you have conquered. Truth, like a white angel, stood on one side of you; Cowardice, like a black one, on the other; and, beneath the standard of Mary, truth has prevailed, the white angel has conquered. Are you surprised now that I congratulate you?"

There was another pause, during which Mrs. Glover held her pupil's hand in hers.

"What shall I do? will you tell me, Mrs. Glover?"

"Your duty, dear child, and that rather a difficult one."

Emily shrank for a moment, but she thought of the chapel and her resolution, and felt as strong as a little Crusader.

"First of all, you must undeceive Katie, as you have done me, with regard to your generosity."

"I long to do that."

"And Simpson must no longer suspect any one unjustly. What will you say to her?"

Pride quivered for a moment in every feature of Emily Weston's face. Humble herself to a servant! Impossible! But Mrs. Glover was waiting for an answer.

"What will you say to her?" she asked again. As the sunshine falls on a dark pool, a better thought fell on the shadows of Emily's pride, as her governess whispered the little word *humility*.

"I will tell her the truth," she replied firmly, and that pressure of her hand was a reward in itself.

"With regard to the opening of the window, I will explain that for you in your presence."

"Thank you, thank you, dear Mrs. Glover," cried poor Emily.

"You are only just in time," continued Mrs. Glover. "This very morning I should have given all the servants notice to leave, except Simpson, unless the truth had been told in a week. There is one other thing for you to do, and that is, as soon as we have started this afternoon, to write and ask Father Gilbert for a new measure, saying that you do so at my request, you having destroyed the first, and through carelessness. And now, my dear child, wrong as you have been, I need say no more, for I am convinced that no words of mine could add to a penitence that has been the immediate work of God. Go and do as you have determined, and may God bless you."

The White Angel.   47

Emily went, and, notwithstanding the mortification she had to endure during the ensuing hour, as the knowledge of her fault circled through the house, all were so kind, and her own conscience so light, that by dinner-time there was not a happier child in the school. There was just a little quivering of the lip as the last two girls filed out of the green gates, which swelled into a tear of self-reproach far more bitter as she turned and caught sight of poor Katie, also left behind. But they sat down together in the pretty garden, by Mrs. Glover's permission, as soon as Emily had finished her letter to Father Gilbert, and talked of such bright and beautiful things that Katie forgot her pain, Emily her troubles, and both their disappointment, in the interest of their conversation.

That Thursday was a golden day in Emily's life, and she never forgot it. Little Eva's prayers, Mrs. Glover's kindness, and Katie's advice, stood as a triple tower in the memory of the past, on which she looked back gratefully for many a long year, when none had grown more courageous in the path of duty than Emily Weston.

* . * * * *

There is a nun in a quiet convent far across the sea, sweet Sister Gertrude. How she smiles beneath her long black veil when the roll of the soldier's drum is heard from the distant boulevard.

"Do you like to hear it, Sister Gertrude?"

"Yes, sometimes very much."

"Does it not make you think of battles?"

"Yes, Eugénie, of one battle in particular that was very hard to fight."

"Who won?"

"The White Angel."

"What do you mean, Sister Gertrude? Who was the White Angel, and how did he win the battle?"

"His name was Truth, and he won the battle by Prayer."

Eugénie shook her head over Sister Gertrude's riddle, but I think you could have guessed it, little reader!

MABEL.

CHAPTER I.

THERE was once a little girl, and her name was Mabel. She was a merry, bright little girl, whose sparkling eyes were so full of fun that one could hardly fancy she could ever do anything but laugh. And yet she could look serious, and very serious too in church, for Mabel loved God too well to forget Him as she knelt in His very presence; and she knew, too, that as she lived at the Hall, and had the squire for her papa, that all the village children would look up to her for an example. Nor did her love of fun and play make her forget her duties, but she said her lessons, ran her scales, and hemmed her dusters, as if there had been no such things as sunny days, skipping-ropes, and dolls in existence. Then, again, Mabel was charitable, and her greatest treat was to visit the poor with her mother, though many of them were cross old women who hardly looked at her, or dirty children who stroked her with sticky fingers; and though she had to carry a big basket that a grand young lady in Dublin would never dream of lifting from one chair to another. But Mabel was not a grand young lady, only a good, pious little girl, who was happy when she did right, and sorry when she did wrong, and who was taught her duty towards God and her neighbour in the good old-fashioned way.

Mabel lived in a pretty village, almost hidden in a valley between two hills. The people of the parish were very poor, for though most of them farmed their own little fields, the crops were so very scanty that when their fortunes were brightest, they were very thankful if all their children had shoes and stockings for mass on Sundays, and if they could give them a good dinner when they came home. Still, you could not have found a more contented village between the Irish Sea and the waves of the broad Atlantic.

Poor little Mabel had no companions of her own age, for she was an only child, and the next family lived so far away on the other side of the mountain that she very seldom saw them, so seldom indeed that when the children once in a way came to see her, she felt quite strange and shy, and stood a long time considering what she ought to say first.

Mabel. 51

Now though Mabel knew and loved almost every one in the village, her one great favourite was the parish priest, "big Father John." He was a tall, portly man, with a round red face, and a dingy coat; but those who knew him best, knew that the coat would have been less dingy had the heart beneath it been less warm, while those who remembered his face in the dark days of famine and fever, or who saw it lighted up with enthusiasm as he preached, quite forgot its roundness and ruddiness, and saw in it only the clear bright shining of the love of God. He was so good that Mabel used to wonder how even the great saints could be better, and yet so playful and funny that she could not possibly have had a merrier playfellow. Sometimes when he had finished his game of chess or backgammon with her papa, Mabel would induce Father John to play at beggar-my-neighbour with her, and then I do not believe there was a happier little girl in all Ireland.

Big Father John had not acquired this addition to his name from anything very remarkable in his size or appearance, but the priest of the next parish was also a Father John, and as their surnames chanced to be the same, he on his side was distinguished as "little Father John." Nor were these titles inappropriate, for big

Father John walked with a firm foot, breathed with strong lungs, spoke with a loud voice, and seemed ready to grapple with the three great enemies of mankind till death. Little Father John passed on his way silently, thoughtfully, always praying and suffering, always exhorting and entreating. The zeal of big Father John loved to dwell on the preaching of the Apostles, and the sufferings of the Martyrs, while the love of little Father John seemed to chain him to the foot of the Cross, and he never seemed to stir from its shadow, never to forget for one moment that he was the servant of a crucified Master. Their bishop said that never had he known two holier parish priests.

One bright summer afternoon, Mabel was walking quietly homewards with her large black curly dog. She must have been very deep in thought, for she did not hear a step that came close behind her, and she was quite startled when the joyous voice of big Father John accosted her.

"And where have you been travelling to, little woman, this bright afternoon?"

"Not very far, Father John, only to the village."

"And what has Bob been doing that you leave him to walk all alone with his tail drooping in such a disconsolate fashion? I have been watching you all the way up from the white gate, and I felt quite sorry for the poor fellow."

"Bob! Oh, he has been doing nothing, but he always walks like that, when I don't speak to him."

"Why don't you speak to him, then?"

"So I do generally; but I went this morning with mamma to see little Father John, and I cannot get him out of my head."

"Why not?"

"Because he looks so very pale and ill. Father, do you know I think he will die!"

"So do I, Mabel."

They walked on in silence for some way, and once again Bob looked very forlorn.

"He is to come and stay with us in the autumn. Mamma would not come away till he promised."

"God bless her kind heart. I was afraid she would not be able to persuade him."

The reader must not suppose that big Father John made use of phrases couched in well-turned English. Not at all. I only wish I could give them in their original richness and raciness, for I hate translations. If the reader hates them too, let him (if he can) turn them back into the broadest, best humoured Irish brogue possible, and he will have big Father John to the letter.

"Little Father John has a new servant man," observed Mabel, "so nice and kind. He took me all over the place, and showed me everything."

"Do you mean old Peter?"

"Yes, do you know him?"

"Very well; but you are mistaken, he is not Father John's servant. His is entirely a labour of love, that he considers it the one blessing of his life to be allowed to perform."

"He must love Father John very much."

"He does, any one may know that who sees that tall, haggard figure watching for the first glance of the old housekeeper in the morning. He loves him dearly, and with good reason. I will tell you his story if you like, for it is no secret."

"Please do, Father John."

"Well, then, I think you will hardly believe me if I tell you that twelve months ago if there was a bad, wicked man in the world, it was Black Peter. Did you never hear of him?"

"Black Peter!" echoed Mabel. "Oh, Father John, was I talking to Black Peter?"

"To no other," said Father John, laughing. "Never mind, I would trust him with untold gold now, or even a dozen little Mabels, precious as they would be to us. But in those days certainly Black Peter would have been a sorry guardian. He was the scourge of the country, far and wide. He ill-used his wife, starved his children, robbed his neighbours, blasphemed God, and led many a poor young fellow, who would have done well, into the paths of iniquity. Black Peter was not a Catholic, but little Father John, from the first moment he set foot in that parish, seems to have set his heart on reforming him. The consequence was, that Black Peter hated him from the very bottom of his heart, and did him all the mischief he could. He smashed his windows, barked his trees, and robbed his fowl-house, but these were only trifles to Black Peter. One dark night he waylaid him, and pulled him from his horse; but before he could do him any harm, a couple of sturdy farmers chanced to come up, and Peter decamped, nor was he seen in the place for a long time afterwards. He, however, turned up again in a most unexpected manner. One cold day, little Father John, walking alone by the mill-stream, saw a man's hat floating on the water. Startled by the occurrence, he had hardly re-recovered himself before he perceived the body of a man rise to the surface, and saw at a glance that it was no other than Black Peter. Little Father John knows no more of swimming than you do, but with the loudest shout for help he ever gave in his life, I'll be bound, in he went

He seized the unhappy man just as he was sinking, dashed at the chain of the eel-trap, caught it, and held on till some men came to his assistance. Father John and his charge were soon drawn out of the water, and Black Peter was put to bed at the mill. Not so Father John. He certainly changed his wet clothes as soon as he saw Black Peter restored to consciousness, but that was quite half an hour after the accident. It was with difficulty he could be induced to leave him even for that, for having saved the life of his enemy, his next thought was to save his soul. I am told that the countenance of Peter was something dreadful, when he discovered little Father John in the person of his benefactor. But Father John, with the brightest countenance in the world, seized his hand, patted and stroked it in the most affectionate manner possible, as he talked to the bystanders of how nearly it had been stiffened in death. Then all the miller's family withdrew, and Father John remained alone with this wretched man, who had hitherto scoffed at all religion. God only knows what passed in that solemn interview, but at the end of about an hour Father John called for water, and baptized Black Peter as the miller's family knelt round the bed. Peter was a long time ill, but Father John went again and again to see him, and at last, one morning in May, Black Peter and his ill-used wife knelt side by side in the church, and made their first communion amid the prayers, tears, and thanksgivings of the whole parish. Nor was it a passing excitement with Peter. Like his glorious namesake, his was a true conversion, and Father John has so much faith in his sincerity that he gives him holy communion several times a week."

"How happy he must feel every time he sees Peter there."

"Very happy, Mabel; and yet the world would say he had paid dearly for his happiness."

"How?"

"With his life. Men of little Father John's weak constitution cannot do rash things with impunity. He has been always ailing and suffering from his birth; but, from the time of Peter's recovery, he has been gradually sinking, and now—" Big Father John could say no more, and they walked on again in silence. It was interrupted at last by the child.

"Father John?"

"Yes, my child."

"Do you think it was wrong for little Father John to keep on his wet clothes so long?"

"No, Mabel, because he never could see any virtue in taking care of himself, or he would have done so. His is a holy kind of carelessness, peculiar partly to his character and partly to his disease."

"Then I think I can understand why it all happened," and Mabel looked very earnestly up at Father John.

"Why?"

"Because our Lord wants him in heaven, and so He allowed him to be careless about himself. Don't you think so?"

"Perhaps, Mabel."

"Are you not pleased when you think of that reason? I am."

"Yes," returned Father John, "or at least, Mabel, I try to feel so, and to say from the depths, yes, from the very depths, of my heart, God's will be done!"

"Everybody loves little Father John," said Mabel, musingly—"papa, mamma, Peter, and all his parishioners—even Bob loves him—don't you, Bob? But I think, father, you love him better than anybody else, better even than Peter."

"I love him as my life—my dear, dear old friend!" and, unable to restrain himself any longer, big Father John sobbed like a child; while Mabel was so terrified at the result of her observation, that she walked home all the rest of the way as mute as a mouse.

CHAPTER II.

LITTLE Father John came, as he had promised Mabel's mother, as soon as the autumn winds had tempered the summer heat. Always small and spare, he had now dwindled almost to a shadow, while his face, naturally thin and pale, had grown almost unearthly in its whiteness and attenuation. Strangely in contrast with this emaciation was the speaking energy of his large dark eyes, which still flashed with a zeal and earnestness to be quenched only in death, and his voice, which could still grow deep when he talked of the love of God and resignation. Mabel and Bob were his constant companions as he crept slowly through the beautiful autumnal lanes and woods, where the blackberries hung in rich festoons, and where the scarlet berries of the hawthorn had transformed the hedges into masses of living coral. And as the soft wind swept the dead and dying leaves from the branches, and hurried them along in brisk eddying showers, little Father John talked so beautifully to Mabel of death and resurrection, that the child almost sighed to think that her life was still so green and spring-like, and she looked almost wistfully at the half-green leaves that had done their work so soon, and were falling so peacefully amid the autumn sunshine.

One afternoon big Father John came up to the hall, and the two guests had a long talk all to themselves. It seemed very long to Mabel, who was left alone, for her mamma was busy writing letters, her father out, and Bob as sleepy and stupid as a dog could be. It was rather a sleepy afternoon, for the rain pattered drearily against the windows, and the wind said most dreary, mournful things, Mabel thought, as it howled and moaned among the tree-tops and chimneys. She was, therefore, not at all sorry when she saw a large umbrella gradually disappear down the drive, for she knew that under that umbrella was the sturdy form of the parish priest, and now she might go to little Father John. She accordingly crept quietly into the summer-room, where he was lying on a sofa, propped up by large white pillows; but he was so lost in meditation that neither her footsteps nor the whisking of Bob's heavy tail on the carpet seemed to disturb him. So Mabel took her little chair, and sat at the window watching the rain-drops, and feeling quite dismal and neglected. Then she whispered a long disconnected story to Bob about her mamma's letter, and the bad weather, and of how nobody cared about her at all. If Bob could have answered, he would have said (for he was a sensible old dog), "If little girls sit still and do nothing for

Mabel.   61

a whole afternoon, they must expect to feel dismal. If you had hemmed one of your papa's new silk handkerchiefs, you would have been as happy as I am," and Bob's tail would have wagged in demonstration of his canine contentment. I think, as it was, Mabel's guardian angel must have whispered a tiny little word or two, for she rose from the chair, found the handkerchief, and her thimble, and her fingers were soon moving quite as fast as Bob's tail.

But after a time it began to grow dark, and though Mabel stitched on as long as she could, she was obliged to give it up at last. Little Father John had not stirred once, so Mabel sat very still and watched the heavy black clouds that were driving rapidly across the sky. She was not at all cross or unhappy now; still everything looked so mournful outside, that she could not help feeling rather sad. She sat and thought of the great wide world she had never seen, with its busy cities, and tangled forests, its palaces and garrets, its famines, fevers, and battle-fields, and all the men, women, and little children, who were wandering about it, suffering, rejoicing, working, and dying. For Mabel's mother had often talked to her of these things, and had told her that a little girl in a far-away village forms part of a great bustling crowd of people, that every man was her brother, and that in a world of sin and suffering no one must live for himself. How many more sad things Mabel would have thought about I cannot tell you, but just at this moment a servant came quietly in, with the welcome news that she was to light a fire, because the evening was too chilly for the father, God bless him. So Mabel and Bob watched Betty lay the sticks, and pile on the turf, and a glorious bright fire was soon blazing and dancing up the chimney, as only turf fires can blaze and dance. And then Father John was wheeled beside it, and Mabel brought her little chair and sat at his feet, while Bob stretched himself full length, blinked his eyes at it, and reckoned himself the happiest dog in Ireland.

"You are a good quiet little nurse, Mabel," said the priest, at length; "if I had not seen you come in, I should not have known you were in the room."

"Did you see me, father? I thought you were asleep."

"No, I was thinking over all the bright and beautiful things Father John has been saying to me, God bless him. What were you doing all the time you were so still?"

"Hemming papa's handkerchief, and then I was thinking."

"What about?"

"A great many things, father."

"Tell me some of them."

"I don't think I could, because I did not know I was thinking, and so I forget."

Father John smiled, "Tell me the last thing."

"Oh, the last thing, I was wondering how what mamma said the other day could be true."

"What was it?"

"She said that every thing in the world is of some use."

"And don't you think she was right?"

"Why, Father John, what good are children?"

"Of as much good as men and women, Mabel, if they do their duty."

"Of what good am I? Mamma could do all I do in the whole day, in half an hour."

"That is very likely, still you are one of the little bricks that God is using in building up the great temple of His Providence. And if you learn your lessons, hem your papa's handkerchief, or look after a poor sick little man like me, you are doing the work God destined you to do from the beginning of the world, work that in fact He created you to do; and if you were to die to-morrow, and had done only such things as these in your young life, but perfectly, with God's help, and for God's sake, you would fly straight up, and take your place among

God's own saints, and find one of the brightest crowns in heaven waiting for you. Then, besides, you must remember that there would be no roses if there were no buds, and we hope some day you are going to grow up into a tall wise woman, and spend a long lifetime in God's service."

Mabel smiled.

"It is astonishing," continued Father John, "how much actual good little people can do. During a great part of the time I have been lying here, I have been thinking of the great and wonderful works of one child's life—works that, I trust, in the mercy of God, will bear fruit throughout eternity. Some day, perhaps, I may tell you his story."

"Not now, father?" and Mabel's look was a very pleading one.

"Well, stir the turf, and give me ten minutes, and then we will see," said Father John, opening his breviary.

Little Father John's ten minutes were a good half-hour. Mabel said her rosary, and then shaped things in the turf very patiently, but she could not help a tiny little sigh when the minute-hand commenced its travels round the other half of the clock-face. Father John heard it, and the book was shut in an instant.

"And so I am to tell you a story, am I,

Mabel?" He thought for a few moments, and a strange expression stole over his face that the child remembered in after years. "Very well," he exclaimed at length, and then, to Mabel's delight, commenced his story in the way that stories have begun since the days of the Flood.

"There was once a little boy who lived in a great city, who had many comforts and kind friends, and who ought to have been very happy."

"His father must have been rich, then?"

"Well, yes, he was."

"Very rich?"

"Yes, I suppose so."

"What was the little boy's name?"

"Johnnie."

"Was he good?"

"No; peevish, selfish, and ungrateful to God and his parents."

"What a naughty boy!"

"That he certainly was, for though they used to buy him all sorts of books and playthings, nothing satisfied Master Johnnie. He was always discontented."

"Well, but, father," chimed in Mabel, who began to feel rather uncomfortable, "I get tired of toys too, sometimes. Wouldn't they let him go out and run about?"

"He certainly had a slight excuse for some

F

of his bad tempers, Mabel, but it was very slight indeed. He was so delicate that he rarely stirred out of the house in the winter, and even in the summer he could not run about like other children."

"Poor Johnnie, no wonder he was naughty! Was his mother good?"

"Yes," said the priest, and his voice seemed to change, "very good in some things, but she had been taught to love the world. Johnnie saw little of her in his childhood, for she was obliged to go out a great deal, and he had to be left to the charge of people who paid attention to his comforts and education, but who found it less troublesome to gratify his whims than to regulate his mind."

"Had he any brothers and sisters?"

"Yes, but all the children that had come between them and him were dead, and so they were all much older."

"Where was his father?"

"Dead; and they had loved each other so dearly, that the thought of him was a very sad one to the little boy."

"Had he no companions?"

"No; children of his own age did not care to be with a sullen, sickly boy, who always wanted his own way. So he was left very much to himself, and often read more rubbish in one day than I hope you will read in your whole life. When he was tired of reading he used to sit at the window that looked down from a great height on a wide, bustling street, and at night he used to creep to the top of the broad staircase and listen to the music below, and wonder if he should ever grow up and see the great people, as his brother and sisters did. When he was about eleven years old his brother came of age, and his sisters left school and went out into the great world with their mother, and they were obliged to leave Johnnie more alone than ever. Now, though he was so naughty as to repine, and think hard things about his relations, God took pity upon him, and sent the little ungrateful boy a friend."

"Was he young?"

"Yes, about his own age, but half as big again."

"Was he rich?"

"No, poor."

"Very poor?"

"Yes, but with that bright, clean, holy poverty the saints love so much."

"What was his name?"

"John."

"Two Johns! How funny! Was he good?"

"As good as he was poor," said the priest, fervently.

"How came Johnnie to know him?"

"In rather an odd way. Johnnie's window, which had a side view of the street, commanded two small shops, one of which was kept by a newsman. Now in this place there was a certain errand boy that used to inspire Johnnie with a large amount of interest. Indeed, he watched him so often that he knew the hours of his rounds, of his meals, of his shop-sweeping, and of all the other etceteras that go to make up an errand boy's life. Johnnie found out other things about him too; for instance, that he was honest and good-natured, for once he saw him run after a lady who had dropped her purse, and at another time he saw him help an old woman to gather up the apples another boy had knocked over, and that even after the old woman had boxed his ears by mistake; and when she gave him two rosy apples, by way of reparation and gratitude, Johnnie saw him give them to his two little brothers, who came to fetch him home to dinner. All this was so interesting, that at last Johnnie took more pleasure in watching this newsboy, with his round, red face, and coarse hands, his patched jacket, and woollen comforter, than in following the fortunes and adventures of the most beautiful lords and ladies that were ever written about. As the winter came on, Johnnie could see the chilblains on his blue-red fingers, even from where he sat, and almost shivered himself when he saw him turn out in the biting cold with his bundle of papers and books. If anybody had asked Johnnie whom he most pitied in the world, he would have said the boy at the news-shop.

"Now, it seems that all this time, as the newspaper boy bustled about his work, he thought very often during the day of a certain little pale face that looked out for so long together upon the moving crowd below. Sometimes he saw him, still just as sad and lonely-looking, drive off in a carriage full of bright ladies; and if he had been asked whom he pitied most in the world, he would have pointed to the high window, and said, the little sickly gentleman up there.

"One day Johnnie saw the paper-boy examining a small clumsily-carved boat with great attention, and from that moment was seized with a great desire to give him a handsome little ship that he chanced to possess. Do not, however, suppose he would have been so generous had he wanted it himself; but, as I told you, he had plenty of toys. Now it seems that the paper-boy, on his side, had made a scrapbook out of some old illustrated periodicals his master had given him, and he often thought how it would amuse the young gentleman who went out so seldom. One morning, therefore, when he left the newspaper, he ventured to give it to the servant; and as the man was good-natured, he took it up to Johnnie, with a very respectful message from the little boy. The result was that the newsboy was taken up into Johnnie's room, who showed him the boat, but as the other could not spare time to receive the explanation of its various parts and contrivances, he was invited to come during his spare time. He came, and a life friendship dated from that evening, for Johnnie's mother, hearing that her child's face brightened at the step of his new friend, encouraged John's visits, as soon as she had satisfied herself of his respectability and worth; and of all the actions of her life, and she did many wise ones in after years, this was perhaps one of the wisest.

"Johnnie's discontent often led him to commit grave sins. Amongst others, that of murmuring against his mother was not infrequent. This spirit he generally kept to himself, and brooded over it in silence; but one day, fancying himself more than usually aggrieved, he told John his troubles, and ended by asking his advice.

"'What would you do, John, if your mother told you that you must not do something you had set your heart upon?'

"'I should not do it, Master Johnnie, of course.'

"'But if you wished to do it very much?'
"'I should think of the house at Nazareth.'
"'What for?'
"John looked surprised.
"'I don't know what you mean,' said Johnnie. 'What has a house to do with the question? Who lives there?'
"'Our Lord and His Blessed Mother lived there once,' said John, simply. 'He was Almighty God, you know, and yet, though the Blessed Virgin was His own creature, He obeyed her in every little thing. We have not much merit in obeying our mother after that, I think.'
"Johnnie was silent for a few minutes. 'I am tired of obeying mine,' he said at length, 'and as for my brother, I hate him?'
"'Master Johnnie!'
"'I do. Always treating me like a baby, because he happens to be twenty-one. Wouldn't you hate him if you were me?'
"'No, Master Johnnie, I should think of our Blessed Lord upon the Cross, and then I should not dare to hate my enemies, much less my brother!'
"'How strangely you talk, John! I never heard a boy say such queer things, it seems like church! I don't like to think and talk about such things as these, do you?'
"'Yes, Master Johnnie.'

"'Well, perhaps I might too, if I knew more about them.'

"'But you do know, Master Johnnie; you know all about our Lord being born in Bethlehem, and the angels and the shepherds, and the ox and the ass; and John told in simple words the story of the Incarnation.'

"'Go on,' said Johnnie, and pulling the other down beside him on a sofa, he leaned his poor little weary head against him and listened. And so John told him of the flight into Egypt, and the long silent life at Nazareth.

"'Go on,' said Johnnie.

"It was dark outside and growing late, but the two boys clung together in the flickering firelight, and John spoke in words more burning than he has ever spoken since, of Gethsemane and Calvary. It was a long story, and at the words of that last bitter cry, Johnnie wept as if he, too, had stood beneath the Cross.

"'Is it true, quite true, John?'

"'The very truth,' and the arm of the working lad clasped the spoiled boy of fortune to his heart. There were preparations below, and knock after knock thundered through the house, but the two boys sat in a soft, dreamy stillness.

"'I wish I had lived there, John, I would have tried to save Him from the Jews.'

"'It could not be, Master Johnnie, because,

you see, if our Blessed Lord had not died, we must all have been lost;' and John went on till the doctrine of man's redemption was shaped out clear and bright. Then he told the other about the Resurrection, and Johnnie thrilled with joy. But he trembled while he listened, as the story went on, for fear the heavenly Guest should depart and leave the world once more in shadow. The moment came, and like 'the men of Galilee,' Johnnie gazed up into heaven after his departed Lord, and once more wept on his companion's shoulder.

"'Did He go for ever?' he asked.

"'No, Master Johnnie;' and with childish lips, in childish words, he poured into childish ears the mystery of the Altar. Had it come in later years, Johnnie would have met it with doubts and arguments, but falling as it did, in its own natural sequence, to the Sacrifice of the Cross, the two truths came at the same time and with the same force, never to be separated, never to be doubted. A servant came in, the fire was stirred, and the candles lighted, and the conversation changed. But a bond had been woven between those two young hearts never to be broken. No, never," continued little Father John, with deep emotion, "for death, that severs all earthly ties, shall only draw that more closely!

"Time went on, and the two boys grew more than ever attached, although John's visits were rare, for his hours were long, and his strong sense of duty kept him strictly to them. But the Sundays were his own, and the greater part of these were passed in the dull monotony of Johnnie's room.

"'John,' said the latter, a few days after their other conversation, 'where do you sit in church?'

"'I don't go to your church, Master Johnnie.'

"'I thought you did; to which one, then?'

"John told him, but the other was none the wiser.

"'Will you go to ours next Sunday?'

"'I can't, Master Johnnie.'

"'Why not? Isn't it as good as yours?'

"John was silent.

"'Ours is very large,' continued John. 'Is yours as big?'

"'Much larger, sir.'

"'Well, ours is very old—a hundred years at least.'

"'Ours is older, sir.'

"'But ours is very beautiful, with grand high pillars, and stained windows. It was built by a very great man.'

"'Ours is beautiful as God can make it, and God built it up Himself.' There was a strange bright look in the round, red face that puzzled Johnnie.

"'What do you mean, John? God never built a church, I'm sure.'

"'Yes, Master Johnnie, he did; built it of men and women, boys and girls. Put seven great pillars in it (as the sermon said this morning), and placed glorious great saints in it for windows, all to give light, and yet all different, like different-coloured glass, with the same sun shining through.'

"'John, I think you are going mad.'

"'No, Master Johnnie, I'm not; but you are talking of one thing, and I of another. You mean a building of stone or brick, and I the great, bright, glorious Church of God. The time has come, Master Johnnie, for me to tell you the truth; it is hard, because perhaps you will send me away, but my religion is not the same as yours, I am a Catholic.'

"'Oh, John, John, I am so sorry! I always thought you were the same as we. My tutor says the Catholic religion is so dreadful! Do turn Protestant!' and, in a state of high excitement, Johnnie poured forth the result of his historical researches. But John stood immovable, and when Johnnie paused, he only smiled very quietly.

"'Will you be a Protestant?' asked Johnnie, winding his arms round his friend's neck.

"'No, Master Johnnie, I would die for the old faith.'

"The other made no reply, and John continued. He spoke of the planting of the Church, and went through the Roman emperors by name and in succession as he spoke of the early Christians, in a way Johnnie could not have attempted. He followed the history of the Church calmly and quietly, as if he had been telling the history of his father's household—and was not this the very history that the boy was telling? When he came to the Reformation, he went through it without colouring or anger, simply and naturally reciting all in its native truth. He spoke of the English heresy, as his own faith saw it, a dark cloud passing across the clear, bright sun, as more transient heresies and schisms had passed before, and showed the future lighted up, as the brilliancy of his own enthusiasm saw it, with the triumph of the ancient faith.

"'Where did you learn all this, John?' asked his listener.

"'Only from hearing sermons, and reading the library books, Master Johnnie.'

"'Will you get me some of those books?'

"'Yes, sir.'

"John kept his word, and from that day Johnnie read no more rubbish."

"He seems to be getting good, father," observed Mabel.

"He could not help getting better with so saintly a lad as John for his companion, whose every word and example was a check on his selfishness, indolence, and discontent. But he never became good. Ah, no, my child, he never became good!"

"Poor Johnnie! Go on, please, Father John."

"Well, Mabel, it would be impossible for me to tell you all the grave conversations that passed between these two boys, or the intense admiration and respect with which the poor boy inspired the rich one as they grew older. Johnnie seemed to live in another world, for the burning words of his friend were always ringing in his ears, until death, judgment, heaven, and hell became terrible realities. Weak and frail as he was, he learned at last to love God."

"Really, father?"

"Yes, Mabel, that is to say, as really and truly as such weakness could."

"Then, father, he did become good?"

"Because he loved God, Mabel? Is it goodness to kiss the hand that saves us from destruction? to listen to the voice that promises peace in the midst of storms? and to bask in that fire and light that can alone give warmth and life to our souls? God can do all things, and He gave many graces to this child; but He also knows all things, and He knows how little he corresponded with them, how little he strove to turn them to account."

"And was he happy, father?"

"Happy and sorrowful both, bearing some faint resemblance, perhaps, to the state of the holy souls. More than happy in his new-born faith, more than desolate in his banishment from the new love of his life. Sunday after Sunday he drove to the fashionable church with his family, day after day he pined for that Presence he had never entered, for the altar he had never seen. At last a tremendous resolution was taken, a momentous question asked, and the answer was the dismissal of his friend.

"Then the white cheek grew whiter, and the thin hands thinner, and at last Johnnie lay on a sick-bed. And then there was a hurrying to and fro of the whole household. Day and night the mother sat by her child's bedside; his sisters stole in and out of the room on tip-toe, and spoke in whispers; and the big brother that Johnnie had thought so hard, stroked his hair, and peeled his oranges, and promised him no end of things when he should get well. But Johnnie heard very little of all this. The thought of the glorious Presence grew greater every day, and the weight of that weary banishment was crushing him to the grave.

"At last the doctor spoke, 'Young as this child is, the disease is mental.'

"Then the mother bent lovingly down to the little boy, and into her ear, now thrilling with sympathy, Johnnie poured his troubles. She had never guessed that her refusal had caused his illness, and the instant she learned the truth, a messenger was despatched, and in less than ten minutes Johnnie's friend was once more beside him. Then there was a brief, hurried consultation between the lady and the errand boy, and John disappeared. He returned with one who was from that moment the guide of Johnnie's life, and before many minutes the dark shadow that had rested on the child's soul for two long weary years had passed away for ever. Yes, for ever!" added little Father John fervently, "for though other shadows may have fallen afterwards, they were light indeed compared with that bitter separation."

"Do you mean, father, that Johnnie's mother let him become a Catholic?"

"Yes, Mabel, and never from that moment interfered with his religion, though her not doing so incurred the censure of all her friends and relations. Of course, by his companion's advice, he was careful not to annoy her with it, and so she let him go to church where he liked, and spend all the spare time that was at John's disposal with him."

"He got well, then?"

"Yes, quite well, and even pretty strong."

"And fat?"

"No," said the priest, laughing, "never fat, but so well that he was able to go to a very early mass with John every morning, while before his illness they had had a great deal of trouble to get him out of bed by eleven."

"I wonder how he felt the first time he went to mass?"

The answer was long in coming, for little Father John pressed his hands over his face, and lay still so long, that Mabel thought the story must be ended. "If ever you and he get to heaven, Mabel," he said at length, "perhaps he will tell you; as for me, I know no language that would describe such happiness.

"Years went on, and side by side the two lads grew up to manhood. Bright and sunny years to look back upon, and yet, like the years of other men's lives, these too, of course, were checkered with sunshine and shade. Yet, on the whole, the boys were happy, very happy, John taking rapid strides on the road to heaven, the other limping feebly in his track."

"Did John always stop at the newspaper shop?"

"Oh no. At eighteen he became clerk in a lawyer's office, and at three-and-twenty had risen so high in his master's favour, that people began to foretell great things of his future prospects."

"How came he to get on so well?"

"Oh, as to that, he had some friends who helped him."

"And Johnnie?"

"He went to college, and of course received a grand education, for which he was never properly grateful."

"Was he as clever as John?"

"As clever as John! No, not a hundredth part, and yet he thought himself somebody very grand in those days, I can tell you. Things went on quietly for a short time after Johnnie left college, and then quite suddenly a splendid prospect opened before them both. Johnnie's mother procured him a first-rate appointment in India, and John's master, Mr. Raikes, announced his intention of presenting him with his articles, having found him, as he phrased it, an honest, talented, modest, industrious, high-principled young fellow."

"How pleased they must have been!"

"Yes; they received the news on the same

G

day, and that evening strolled out together for a country ramble. Ever since the morning, congratulations had been ringing in their ears, and, for that reason, perhaps, they did not care to congratulate each other. They seemed both disposed for silence, and for the first half-hour hardly a word was spoken. At last they reached a churchyard, and, as they seated themselves on the gate, their eyes met, and both saw a troubled look on the other's face.

"'We shall think of these evenings in days to come, John.'

"'Yes,' said John.

"'When we are great men, perhaps. Eh, John?'

"John smiled, and sighed.

"'One "His Excellency" and the other on the woolsack. Eh, John?'

"Again John smiled.

"'Supposing even that could come to pass, would you wish for it?'

"'Would you?' asked John, turning suddenly, and laying his hand gently on his friend's.

"The ice was broken, and the two young men sat, as they had done so many years ago, and each revealed his trouble to his friend. It was a holy confidence, for that night each crushed the last whisper of ambition. When the bell tolled the people in for the evening rosary, the two young men followed, and two young hearts were that night consecrated to God for ever before the altar of Mary."

"Did they both become priests, father?"

"Yes, my child."

"And what did Johnnie's mother say?"

"She wept for joy."

"For joy!"

"Yes, Mabel, for by that time she and all her family were Catholics."

"And did she still love the world and go about visiting?"

"Yes, she still loved the world, but for God's sake, and she still went out visiting, and her friends were the poor, the sick, and the sorrowful. She lived long enough to hear her boys say mass, and died the death of the just."

"And Johnnie's brother?"

"He married and went abroad, and is bringing up a large family in the fear of God."

"And his sisters?"

"Are both religious, Mabel. Did I not speak the truth when I said I would tell you of a boy that had done great and glorious things?"

"And, father, did Johnnie?—"

"Here comes your mother, my dear child, and I think, as I am tired, that must do for to-night."

CHAPTER III.

It was a cold winter night, the snow was falling and driving heavily, and the wind howling fiercely through the fir-wood and across the hills. It was a fit night to draw down the curtains and heap on the turf, and to make people who were inside feel very sorry for those who were out. Round the bright fire at the hall sat the squire and his wife, big Father John, and Mabel, and very sad they were, though their faces wore a calm, resigned look. They were talking very quietly, and Mabel sat on the floor, with Bob's big rough head in her lap, listening to their low hushed voices, and thinking of sadder things than she had ever thought of in her life before, for death and a black frock were new things to Mabel.

"Did little Father John ever tell you the story of the two Johnnies?" she asked, suddenly looking up.

"What was it, Mabel?" asked the priest.

"A story about a rich boy and a poor one."

"What about them?"

"The poor one was good, and the rich one—"

"Well, go on."

"I couldn't quite understand. I liked him so much, and yet Father John said he was not good."

"Simply on the principle, then, that 'humility is truth.' Not even the greatest saints are good before God; but compare this rich boy with the rest of mankind, and he was the holiest creature I ever knew."

"Did you know him, then, father?"

"Yes, Mabel, more nearly and truly than his own mother. Knew how he sprang forward into the great arms of God at the first little whisper of His voice, and clung to that God, though bigotry, worldliness, and ambition did their best to snatch him from Him. It was I alone who knew how he stretched out a helping hand, even in his childhood, to a poor, friendless, struggling lad; and how, when they grew older, he educated that boy, and pushed him forward with the money that was allowed him for his own pleasures. Who but he encouraged him by his words, inspired him by his example, and shamed him into action by his patience and resignation? Many admired him, a few understood him, all loved him, but I alone of all the world knew his worth, so silent was his life."

"And did you know the poor boy?"

"Very imperfectly; if I knew him well, I should be the wisest man in the world," returned Father John, with a spark of his natural drollery.

"And where are they now?"

There was a long silence, but Mabel fixed her eyes on the priest and waited for an answer.

"One has gone home," said big Father John at last. "You followed the worn-out body, and laid it to rest among his people, across the hills, this very morning. Faith, Hope, and Charity softly whisper that his soul has gone to God. The other must bide his time, and teach little Mabel how to go to heaven."

OLD MORGAN'S ROSE-TREE.

CHAPTER I.

YES, there he sat on his work-bench, with his clean face and dirty leather apron, his patched jacket and withered hands, his grey locks and sunny smile, a happy, joyous, little old man. How they sang, to be sure, he and his canary, just as though Care had passed them by in her travels, having forgotten two such insignificant little beings altogether! But it was not so, for her hand not many years ago ploughed those long wrinkles on the old cobbler's cheek, and many a silvery thread has she mingled with the old man's wiry hair. Why was he so happy, then, for mending old shoes all day is certainly not the merriest occupation in the world, especially when the sky is very blue above, and loaded hay-carts keep passing to and fro past one's very door? Do you want to know, little reader? shall I tell you why? There was a treasure in old Morgan's heart, deep, deep down, a secret treasure, that made all labour light, all bitterness sweet—and that was the love of God; there was a light in old Morgan's eye, that would have made all things around him seem bright and glowing, even if the summer sun had not been shining there in all its glory, and that was the thought of Heaven. So he stitched, stitched away, and the time flew so fast that he was quite surprised when the village clock struck five, and he recollected that he had not had his tea.

Old Morgan's shop or room—for I really do not know which you would have called it—was very small and bare, but clean and tidy, and on a little rickety table close beside his bench, there stood one of the most beautiful rose-trees you ever saw in your life; so you see we have soon reached the subject of our story, for it was to be about old Morgan's rose-tree. I thought it best to begin by telling you all about it at once.

Simon Morgan was the only cobbler in the pretty little village of Cressendale. He had not always been poor and shabby as we saw him just now; there was a time when he owned a nice shoemaker's shop in the town of D., and had a good wife, and two lovely children. But hard times came, the smart shop was shut up, for Morgan failed, and soon after, his wife and little ones lay beneath the wooden cross that marks their humble graves in the Catholic churchyard of D. Poor old Morgan! He always smiled, though, when he talked of them, for he only thought of them as part of the treasure that lay waiting for him in heaven.

The old Squire of Cressendale had died about a year before our story begins. Though the loss of their kind old friend was deeply felt and lamented, it was nevertheless with shouts of heartfelt joy that the villagers had welcomed home their new master and his bride, on the Christmas Eve afterwards. Many were the rejoicings that followed their arrival, many the plans proposed by young Squire Trevor for the improvement and benefit of his tenantry. Amongst others he arranged a kind of rural flower-show to be held the following summer, and offered a prize, consisting of two sovereigns and a complete set of garden tools, to whoever should raise the most perfect rose-tree, to be presented in full flower. The judges were to be two florists selected by the villagers from a neighbouring town, and two friends of his own, wonderfully skilled as amateur gardeners.

For some weeks past the village had been in a state of great expectation and excitement, that is to say, that portion of it who intended to try for the squire's prize, and beautiful and varied were the roses that were being tended with every kind of attention. I really think the babies must have been jealous, their fathers seemed to think so very little about them! A passing chirrup, or a wave of the big brown hand, was all they had had for many a day, and now that the evening before the show had positively arrived, many of them had to do even without that. Oh, those roses! How proud they would have been if they could only have known the commotion they were creating! But they only unfolded their buds, and spread out their red, white, or pink leaves to the sun, and never troubled their pretty sleepy heads about either the prize or the jealous babies.

Of course every one who was going to try for this prize made sure his rose would win it, though if anybody who understood the matter had taken a sly peep at the plants, he would have been sure that not more perhaps than half a dozen stood any chance of gaining it. The worst of this choice few was certainly not the pink rose that stood beside old Morgan while he and his canary sang, for his father had been a gardener, and few people understood the culture of roses better than the old cobbler.

There was, however, another person in the village whose chance of the prize was by no means a poor one, and this was Harry Rushton.

Old Morgan's Rose-Tree. 91

He was the only son of a respectable farmer in the neighbourhood, who had striven to give him the best education he was able, and to train him up in habits of piety, honesty, and industry; nor did Harry in any way appear likely to disappoint the bright expectations his father had formed concerning him. He was a general favourite, and made his way to hearts that hitherto had looked shyly on those of his religion, for Mr. Rushton's family, like Simon Morgan, were among the few who worshipped God in the good old way, in the little village of Cressendale. Father Stewart was very fond of Harry, and frequently cited both the boy of twelve and the cobbler of many years, as examples worthy to be copied by the young and old of his flock.

The same sonorous stroke of five that had bade old Morgan fill his kettle, had fallen likewise on Harry's ear, just as he reached the green with his satchel on his shoulder; and he mended his pace, knowing that he had loitered in the summer heat, and that his parents prided themselves no little on the punctuality of their meals. Very few minutes saw him seated at the tea-table, busily engaged in satisfying their curiosity concerning his day's lessons, and his own hunger from a plate of very substantial bread-and-butter. Before the meal was ended, a neighbouring farmer dropped in, and the conversation, as a matter of course, turned upon the morrow's gala, and the flower-show.

"There's a sight for you!" exclaimed Farmer Newcome, suddenly observing the flowers in the window-sill. "Ah, Harry, my lad, it'll take a power of posies, I'm thinking, to beat those!"

A gratified smile lighted up the boy's countenance. "I'm glad you think they look well, Mr. Newcome, for they have given me no end of pains and trouble."

"That they have," chimed in his mother. "The first thing in the morning and the last thing at night, there he is bothering over those flowers."

"But don't they pay him for his trouble?" asked his father.

"Why, yes: they do him great credit, though I say so," replied Mrs. Rushton.

"Stop till he gets the Squire's two pounds, and then see if they don't pay him for it!" cried Farmer Newcome, laughing.

"Well, we won't begin to count our chickens too soon, will we, my lad?" observed Mr. Rushton, patting his son on the back; "there are other fine roses besides Harry's in Cressendale."

Harry began to fidget about on his chair, he did not like that speech at all.

"Only this morning I heard a person say,

who is a very good judge in these matters," continued the father, "that there is a rose-bush in the village that would beat any one in the county."

"Whose is that?" asked his three hearers in a breath.

"Do tell us, father, please," said Harry, finding that Mr. Rushton was amusing himself with their curiosity.

"Simon Morgan's."

"Father!" said Harry.

"Stuff and nonsense," cried Mrs. Rushton. "What, that slip of a thing he keeps in his shop?"

"Just so," replied her husband.

"Well!" cried Farmer Newcome, "that beats all I ever heard! I don't pretend to know much about such things—a bunch of turnips would be more in my line—but just don't tell me that a bit of a bush like Morgan's, with about half a dozen flowers on it, is going to beat plants like those, because that just goes against one's common-sense, that does!"

Harry looked as if he thought so too.

"We shall see," said Mr. Rushton; "of course, I shall be glad, delighted, if our boy wins the prize, but I am afraid of his setting his heart too much upon it, and being disappointed, that's all."

Harry stole a glance at his darlings. "They are enough to make one feel confident," thought he, "they must win the prize."

He repeated this over and over again, and when he looked at his mother and Farmer Newcome, their ideas on the subject were evidently so encouraging that he went to bed quite reassured; and yet, somehow, the thought of a little pink rose-tree stole like a shadow over his dreams all night long.

CHAPTER II.

THE gala so long expected was over, the Chinese lamps had burned out, the park was deserted, and the white tents that had been so joyously thronged all day stood silent and ghost-like in the moonlight. The lights in the village kept popping out one by one, but a candle was burning in a lower room, and as the check curtain was not yet lowered, the interior of the little apartment was clearly visible from the street. An old man was standing by the mantel-shelf, with a very pleased look upon his face, and piled against the whitewashed wall all round him, new and bright, were a spade, rake, hoe, and all the etceteras of a complete gardening set. It was the cobbler, who every now and then looked at his new treasures, especially at the two shining sovereigns lying in his withered palm, as though he half doubted the reality of his senses, and was wondering whether his good fortune was not after all a dream.

"Lie there till you are wanted," he exclaimed at length, as he raised his crucifix from the chimney-piece, and placed the money under its stand, "lie there till you are wanted. God only knows when that will be, and Simon does not care how soon; but all in His own good time—all in His own good time!"

He did not change his position for several minutes, but stood looking at his crucifix very earnestly, although his usual hour for bed had gone by some time.

"This will never do, though," he cried at length, rousing himself from his reverie. "I shan't wake in time to get my work done, so as to get to mass to-morrow morning," and he took up and examined a pair of ploughboy's shoes, very unpromising even to a cobbler. "I said they're hardly worth doing," said he, stroking his chin thoughtfully. "But we shall see; poor fellow, he will find it hard to get another pair, I'll warrant. I must do the best I can with them." So saying, he put the shoes on his bench, and commenced his night prayers.

He was very earnest, very intent, for Morgan was seldom troubled with distractions, but poured forth every power of his simple soul in the fervour of his child-like faith—just as you do, I hope, little reader, when you kneel at night by the pretty white-curtained bed! But he did not kneel quietly long, for a sudden crash and the falling of broken glass made him start up pale and breathless to his feet. Poor old man! His courage had passed with the strength of his muscles and sinews, and he trembled like a child. When he turned to examine the extent of the damage, he found a pane of his little window shattered, and two of his beautiful roses lying on the ground beside a sharp stone. No longer alarmed, but deeply grieved, Morgan opened the door and looked up and down the street; but though the moon shone brightly, making every part of it light as day, nobody was to be seen. Having bolted his door, and gathered up his roses, the cobbler finished his prayers, and then, in spite of his recent fright, forgave his enemy, whoever he might be, and slept the sleep of an honest man.

There was a little bed, however, in Cressendale, on which the sleeper slumbered anything but peacefully, and that was Harry Rushton's. Notwithstanding his father's warning, he had felt certain of the prize; and when he learned that it had been awarded to the cobbler, his mortification knew no bounds. He was standing laughing and chatting in high spirits with a group of village lads, when the news of Simon's success reached him, and his transport of rage and envy on hearing of it was anything but edifying to his Protestant companions, who first compassionated, then laughed at him, and finally walked away, leaving him to his ill-humour. Left alone, he wandered to a small wood that bounded the park, and, seating himself upon a block of timber, began to brood over his disappointment. Of course, to a boy of his years this was one of no small extent. The money had never entered into his calculations, because he had intended to give it to his father to lay by with his own savings; but the tools— How he had reckoned upon those! And the fame!— only imagine a boy of twelve carrying off the prize! But now—it was too hard to think about patiently, and Harry sobbed with passion. The taunts of the village boys still rang in his ears, and forgetting how he had provoked them by his surly way of receiving their sympathy, he felt ready to resent them by any means, and at any cost. As for Simon Morgan, he hated him! And yet he had never had, through all his childhood, a warmer, kinder friend. Drawn to him by Simon's kindliness of manner, their common faith had linked them more closely still, and the parents, observing the old man's affection for their child, and esteeming the

H

worthiness of his character, had cultivated his friendship, notwithstanding the difference of position between the farmer of Heathfield and the village cobbler, and Simon Morgan often ate his Sunday's dinner with the Rushtons, and carried home a bunch of Harry's stocks and sweetwilliams to adorn his little cottage. But all this was forgotten, as the full tide of anger and envy swept through poor Harry's heart, and while the bitter tears flowed fast the pink rose and its good old owner met with many an unkind wish.

The evening wore on; the sun began to set behind the old red manor-house, and the laughing and whooping of the village children grew louder and merrier still. Soon the Chinese lamps began to twinkle among the trees, and notwithstanding his bad temper, Harry felt some little curiosity to see them, besides which he knew that his parents would soon begin to wonder where he was; so, drying his eyes, he rose from his mossy seat. It was very peaceful, very quiet; quieter still it seemed, perhaps, because of the distant bustle; just the spot to give one's thoughts to God, if only for a passing moment. Did our little boy do this? Did he pray against the dark temper that had seized him? No, little reader. One flickering thought of doing so passed through his mind, one little thought sent per-

Old Morgan's Rose-Tree. 99

haps by his guardian angel, but Harry resisted it, and walked out of the thicket looking at his toes, as angry and envious as ever.

Neither the Chinese lamps nor the wonderful fireworks afterwards had the power to raise Harry Rushton's spirits, but he wandered about among these beautiful sights almost as if he had nothing to do with them. His father and mother tried to cheer him. Father Stewart patted him on the shoulder and asked if he were ill, and young Squire Trevor laughed and wished him better luck next time, telling him that his roses were very fine, and stood next to Mr. Morgan's. But nobody's kindness had any effect upon him, and he was hardly sorry when all was over, and he found himself walking home with his father and mother and the Newcomes. The latter having remembered that a bag had been left at their house by mistake, which Mr. Rushton would want to take to market with him very early the next morning, proposed, as it was a moonlight night, that Harry should run round with them to fetch it. Mrs. Newcome promised to see him safely through the lane, and his father and mother to wait for him at the white gate, just where the road began to get lonely, so he had therefore only the village street to walk down by himself. Though he met nobody all the way, he never thought of feeling afraid, but walked quickly along in the moonlight, thinking over and over again of the story of his troubles.

Presently, just where the street took a turn, he raised his eyes from the pavement, and there before him stood the cobbler's cottage. His light was still burning, just as we saw him, and as the boy approached, through the uncurtained window, right in front of him, stood the detested rose-tree. A fit of ungovernable fury seized him, and picking up a stone that lay in the kennel, he hurled it through the window. The crash, and the sudden appearance of Morgan, who had been hitherto obscured by the tree, brought him instantly to a sense of his situation, and running away as hard as he could, he soon found himself beside his father and mother at the white gate. With a heavy heart and troubled conscience Harry laid down that night on his little bed, and, hot and feverish, rolled about from one side to the other till his mother came to wake him with her usual morning kiss.

No night prayers, hurried morning ones, no wonder the poor boy found the walk to school unusually hot and trying, the day's tasks unusually hard, and the master unusually stern and severe. As he walked home after the afternoon school, he began to wonder whether he should ever have another happy day, he felt so thoroughly wretched and miserable. He liked nothing: the sunshine, the dust, the children that he met, all were disagreeable, all seemed to mock him in his unhappiness; and though it was somewhat out of his way, he cleared hedges and ditches, climbed gates and fences, until he found himself in the quiet little nook where he had stayed so long the night before. He sat down upon the same mossy bank, with the joyous birds singing over his head, and the shadows of the tall trees falling like a fretwork pavement all around him, and began to think. Of what? Not as he had thought last night, in the bitterness of his soul, of his disappointment, but of his grievous sin, his kind old friend, and the God whom he had offended. Then came tears quite different to those of the night before, tears of real sorrow and repentance; and falling upon his knees among the flickering shadows, he made a true, deep, earnest act of contrition, with a determination to confess his sin as soon as possible, and to make all the reparation in his power for the mischief he had done. Then he shouldered his books once more, and though a task very trying and humiliating to his pride and self-love lay before him, he tripped home, over the grass of Squire Trevor's park, just like Harry Rushton.

CHAPTER III.

"THE very one I was wishing to see, Harry," exclaimed Simon Morgan, as young Rushton entered the old man's cottage about seven o'clock the same evening.

"And I want to see you too, Mr. Morgan," replied Harry, with some trepidation in his voice.

"Do you? that's right, my boy, always glad to see you, and more pleased still when I can do anything for you. Sit down and tell me all about it, but first of all, how are they at home?"

"Very well, thank you; father told me to give you his best respects, and mother has sent you this pot of honey. She says it's out of the new hive, and she thought you would just like to taste it."

There was something more than a taste in the heavy pot that Harry handed the old man.

"Many thanks, many thanks, so I should. O Harry! Harry! you are all too good to me!"

An accusing flush overspread the boy's sunburnt face, unseen, however, by Simon, who was occupied in putting the honey away in his little cupboard.

"And so you won the prize, Mr. Morgan,"

observed his young visitor, at length, as calmly as he could.

"And so I won the prize," said the cobbler, resuming his seat upon his bench, "and very pleased I am about it."

"Do you know, Mr. Morgan, I am a little bit surprised to hear you say so?"

"Are you? Why?"

"Because—I can hardly give you a reason."

"Try."

"Well, because I should have thought you would hardly have cared about such a thing."

"You thought, I suppose, I was too old to care for such a trifle as the credit of growing the best rose in Cressendale."

"No, not too old, it was not that, but I thought somehow that you never cared to make people think much about you."

"How do you mean?"

Harry blushed awkwardly. "Why I mean that I did not think you cared to be praised and talked about, as the whole village is talking about you now."

The cobbler smiled. "You are right, Harry, it was not for the credit's sake that I grew my rose-tree. But the tools were worth trying for, were they not?"

"Why, Mr. Morgan, you have no garden!"

The cobbler laughed outright. "That's true too,

Harry, and yet I wanted to get them; yes, very, very much. But then there was the principal thing of all, there was the money; that will be useful to me, don't you think so?"

"Yes, of course it will, and yet—why you don't generally seem to care for money!"

"Do I not? Well, for all that I was very anxious to get this two pounds, so you see old Simon is more mercenary than you took him to be."

"More what?"

"More mercenary. That is, he loves money, looks at money, thinks about money more than Harry Rushton thought he did, and he is somewhat surprised, eh?"

Harry smiled, but hardly knew what to say; while he was searching for a reply, he gave a side glance at the roses.

It was observed by Morgan. "Ah, Harry, you may well look at them. I was so hot and angry at the time it happened, that I made a resolution not to speak of it till I was cool, but I think I may venture to talk about it now."

Before the sentence was concluded, Harry had crossed the room, and was leaning over the flower as if to examine it, but in reality to hide his tell-tale, burning cheeks.

"What is the matter with it?" he asked in a smothered tone, "it seems all right."

"Does it? Just look there on the mantel-shelf, and at my poor window."

He did look, and two pink roses and a broken pane of glass swam in confusion before him.

"You would hardly think," continued the cobbler, "that I who live such a quiet life here, could have an enemy; and yet, last night, just as I was saying my prayers, a stone was thrown at my poor little plant, right through the window. It ran a very good chance of hitting me too, for I was kneeling just behind it. At first I thought it had something to do with the squire's two sovereigns, and I half wished them back again in his pocket; but as I heard no more, I began to think, and I think still, that the stone was thrown by somebody who was jealous of my winning the prize. I do not wish to begin to consider who it could be, because most likely I should suspect the wrong person; but whoever it was that did it, it was a wicked, cowardly action, don't you think so?"

"Yes I do, indeed I do," cried Harry, with a groan.

"Only fancy," continued Morgan, "to harm a beautiful plant like that, to break a poor man's window, and, to say the least of it, to run the risk of injuring him severely, perhaps even of killing him, for a sharp stone is an ugly thing."

"But, Mr. Morgan, I—he—that is, whoever threw the stone, could not have known you were so near," cried Harry, in an agony of remorse.

"Well, I hope not, my boy, God forbid that I should make the fault worse than it is. As I told you, I was, I daresay, hidden by the rose-bush, but even then there would have been very little excuse for whoever threw the stone; for remember, my lad, no one knows where a stone will fall when it has once left his hand. Ah, Harry, these kind of things come to us through living among those who have not the love of God taught and preached to them, poor souls!"

"But Catholics are wicked too, sometimes, as wicked as they can be!" cried poor Harry.

"Yes, they are, that's true," replied Morgan, "more's the pity that we should have to say so. I would rather, though, lose twenty rose-trees, and have all my windows broken, and my head too, for the matter of that," he added, smiling, "than that one of our people should have done this. There is so little excuse for a Catholic when he commits a wilful and deliberate sin."

My little readers can imagine how every one of the old man's words went to poor Harry's heart. He had entered the cottage on purpose to acknowledge his fault, but cowardice had kept him back at first, and now every moment the task grew more difficult. "Must I tell him?" was the low whisper that kept coming again and again from some little dark corner of his heart.

For some time Simon worked on in silence, absorbed in his own thoughts, and Harry, who had a little recovered his self-possession, stood by his side watching him, without speaking a word. What should he do? "He does not suspect you, and never will; be silent," said the same low whisper. "Pray," said his guardian angel, and Harry prayed.

"I will tell you one reason, Harry, why I am grieved that the beauty of that plant should be in any way spoiled," said Morgan, at length; "I am going to send it up to Father Stewart for the feast of the Sacred Heart. I shall give you a cutting or so, though, first, and then some day perhaps you will be winning a prize. By the by, that reminds me that somebody said you had tried for this one. Is it true?"

"Yes," answered Harry.

"Poor boy! And old Morgan disappointed you. Come, my lad, I will tell you why I wanted the prize, and then I am sure your kind heart will not begrudge it to me. What do you suppose, Harry, has been my greatest earthly dread for years, a thing that I have shrunk from, and have worked early and late to try to prevent?"

"What?" asked Harry, opening his eyes.

"Being buried by the parish! I daresay it is a wrong feeling," cried the old man, excitedly, "I sometimes feel almost as if it were. We ought, I know, to take all the care we can of our souls, and never trouble our heads as to what may become of our poor worn-out old bodies. But I do care, and I can't help it! I was not always poor like this; I knew better days once, and, though I am content with my poverty, and would be contented though I had a hundred times less, still I should like to lie in my own grave, in the one little spot I have chosen in our little churchyard."

"But why did you not tell my father this, or Father Stewart?" asked Harry; "they would have given you the money long ago."

"What! Be buried by charity!" cried the old man; "that would be worse than the parish, for that at least is the pauper's right. But forgive me, Harry; my foolish pride will get the upper hand of me sometimes, even now. No, the Father—God bless him—has plenty of ways for his money, and so has Mr. Rushton, without spending it on the likes of me. Listen! I have saved something myself, and now with that, and those two bright sovereigns of the squire's lying so snugly under his crucifix, old Morgan's last earthly care is over, and he can wait without a pang for death!"

"O Mr. Morgan!" cried Harry, falling on his knees, and seizing the cobbler's hard brown hand in his, "I am so glad, so very glad, you won the prize," and he spoke sincerely.

"God bless you!" cried the old man, stroking the boy's hair with his other hand; "you are a good fellow, Harry; it doesn't always want a large body to hold a large heart. There, there! don't cry, there's a man, but jump up, and run and fetch me those garden things."

Harry obeyed, though very reluctantly, and old Morgan was soon deep in the examination of the tools, which were all that could be desired.

"And so you think these things will not be very useful to me?"

"Not very."

"No, I never thought they would," said the cobbler, "and, therefore, I never intended to keep them. What do you think I am going to do with them?"

"Sell them?"

"Certainly not. What! the squire's gift! No, I am going to do something better than that. I am going to give them to somebody that I truly respect, and because I truly respect him; to somebody who I think loves God to the best of his power, and his neighbour for God's sake. This somebody is not very old, but he sets an example in the village that many older people would do well to follow. You have not yet guessed who I mean?"

"No, I cannot think."

"Harry Rushton."

There was a fierce temptation, a rapid struggle, a brief, fervent prayer, and the danger was over, the victory was won. The young head bowed very low over the old man's hand.

"Mr. Morgan, I broke your window."

There was a silence, only broken by the canary's song, but the wrinkled hand, wet with the child's tears, still lay in his, and another still caressed the smooth brown hair.

"I could not tell you, if I was to try ever so, how miserable I have been ever since last night, or how sorry, how really sorry, I am. God knows both. I know I deserve that you should hate me; but please, Mr. Morgan, do forgive me, for I shall never be happy again unless you do. I felt as if I could have died with shame when I found that it was me you had been praising. And all this misery has been through my wicked, miserable jealousy."

"My child, I do forgive you, and grieve with you from my very heart. You had been sorely tried and tempted, for you had set your heart upon the prize, I see. How I wish you had gained it, my boy! then all this would have been saved."

"Please do not say that," cried Harry, "for I didn't deserve it! I never shall deserve anything good or nice again!"

"Yes, you will; you do even now. You are sorry for your sin; God has forgiven you already, and I am sure I do. The recollection of the temptation and fall will keep you humble, and you will be a better boy than ever."

"I will try, indeed I will."

"And pray!" added the old man, gravely, raising the child's face as he spoke, and quietly kissing his forehead.

"Yes, yes, or I should soon fall again," cried Harry, springing up, and throwing his arms round his old friend's neck.

The sound of a distant bell here broke upon the silence of the little room.

"Will you go with me to Benediction?" asked Morgan.

"Oh, yes, I should like it better than anything in the world."

"Come along then; but bring your tools, we can leave them at Heathfield as we pass."

"Mr. Morgan," said Harry, decidedly, "you must not be offended, but really—really I cannot take them."

"Will you carry them for me, then, as far as Father Stewart's?"

"To be sure I will," and shouldering the prize once so ardently desired, and now so courageously refused, Harry walked along by the old cobbler's side, with a heart as light as the gossamers that floated across their path.

* * * * * *

"Of your charity pray for the soul of Simon Morgan." Yes, there he lies, just where he wished, just where the shadow of the churchyard cross falls in the evening sunset. It is a very peaceful spot, and many a villager loves to linger by the old man's grave, though his colder faith will never bid him pray for the old man's soul. But one who does pray for him comes oftener, much oftener than any one else; comes in moments of doubt and temptation, in moments of hope and joy; comes with the tools that Father Stewart gave him long ago, to trim the lowly grave and the flowers that grow around it. They are very beautiful, and sweet is the perfume they shed over the little graveyard; but sweetest, fairest, most beautiful among them all, is Old Morgan's Rose-Tree.

GEORGE LEVEY, WEST HARDING STREET.

A Select Catalogue of Books

PUBLISHED BY

BURNS, OATES, & CO.,

17 & 18, PORTMAN STREET,

AND

63, PATERNOSTER ROW.

BOOKS LATELY PUBLISHED

BY MESSRS.

BURNS, OATES, & CO.,

17 & 18, Portman Street, and 63, Paternoster Row.

Memorials of those who Suffered for the Faith in Ireland in the Sixteenth, Seventeenth, and Eighteenth Centuries. Collected from Authentic and Original Documents by MYLES O'REILLY, B.A., LL.D. 8vo, 7s. 6d.

"A very valuable compendium of the martyrology of Ireland during the three, or rather two, centuries of active Protestant persecution. The language of many of these original records, written often by a friend or relative of the martyr, is inexpressibly touching, often quite heroic in its tone."—*Dublin Review.*

"Very interesting memories."—*Month.*

Life of St. Thomas of Canterbury. By Mrs. HOPE, Author of "The Early Martyrs" Cloth extra, 4s. 6d.

A valuable addition to the collection of historical books for Catholic readers. It contains a large collection of interesting facts, gleaned with great

BURNS, OATES, & CO., 17, *PORTMAN STREET, W*

industry from the various existing Lives of St. Thomas, and other documents.

"Compiled with great care from the best authors."—*Month.*

"The rich covers of this splendidly-bound volume do not, as is often the case, envelop matter unworthy of its fair exterior. This is a volume which will be found useful as a present, whether in the college or school, for either sex."—*Weekly Register.*

"An agreeable and useful volume."—*Nation.*

"A more complete collection of incidents and anecdotes, combined with events of greater weight, could not be compressed into so compact, yet perfectly roomy, a space."—*Tablet.*

By the same Author.

Life of St. Philip Neri. New Edition.
2s. 6d.; cheap edition, 2s.

NARRATIVE OF MISSIONS.

The Corean Martyrs. By Canon SHORTLAND. Cloth, 2s.

A narrative of Missions and Martyrdoms too little known in this country.

"This is a notice of the martyrs who have fallen in this most interesting mission, and of the history of its rise and progress up to the present day."—*Tablet.*

"No one can read this interesting volume without the most genuine admiration of, and sympathy with, such zeal and constancy."—*Literary Churchman.*

MISSIONARY BIOGRAPHY.

1. *Life of Henry Dorie, Martyr.* Translated by Lady HERBERT. 1s. 6d.; cloth, 2s.

"The circulation of such lives as this of Henry Dorie will do much to promote a spirit of zeal, and to move hearts hitherto

BURNS, OATES, & CO., 63, PATERNOSTER ROW, E.C.

stagnant because they have not been stirred to the generous deeds which characterise Catholic virtues."—*Tablet.*

2. *Théophane Vénard, Martyr in Tonquin.* Edited by the Same. 2s.; cloth elegant, 3s.

"The life of this martyr is not so much a biography as a series of letters translated by Lady Herbert, in which the life of Théophane Vénard unfolds itself by degrees, and in the most natural and interesting way. His disposition was affectionate, and formed for ardent friendship; hence, his correspondence is full of warmth and tenderness, and his love of his sister in particular is exemplary and striking. During ten years he laboured under Mgr. Retord, in the western district of Tonquin, and his efforts for the conversion of souls were crowned with singular success. During the episcopate of his Bishop no less than 40,000 souls were added to the flock of Christ, and Vénard was peculiarly instrumental in gathering in this harvest."—*Northern Press.*

"We cannot take leave of this little volume without an acknowledgment to Lady Herbert for the excellent English dress in which she has presented it to the British public; certainly, no lives are more calculated to inspire vocation to the noble work of the apostolic life than those of Dorie and Vénard."—*Tablet.*

3. *Life of Bishop Brute.* Edited by the Same.

The Martyrdom of St. Cecilia: a Drama. By ALBANY J. CHRISTIE, S.J. With a Frontispiece after Molitor. Elegant cloth, 5s.

"Well-known and beautiful drama."—*Tablet.*

"The receipt of the fourth edition of this beautiful play assures us that our own opinion of its merits has been shared by a wide circle of the Catholic public. The binding is exquisite, and the picture of St. Cecilia is a work of art."—*Weekly Register*

BURNS, OATES, & CO., 17, PORTMAN STREET, W.

The Life of M. Olier, Founder of the Seminary of St. Sulpice; with Notices of his most Eminent Contemporaries. By EDWARD HEALY THOMPSON, M.A. Cloth, 4s.

This Biography has received the special approbation of the Abbé Faillon, Author of "La Vie de M. Olier;" and of the Very Reverend Paul Dubreul, D.D., Superior of the Seminary of St. Sulpice, Baltimore, U.S.

Edited by the Same.

The Life of St. Charles Borromeo. Cloth, 3s. 6d.

Also, lately published, by Mr. THOMPSON.

The Hidden Life of Jesus: a Lesson and Model to Christians. Translated from the French of BOUDON. Cloth, 3s.

"This profound and valuable work has been very carefully and ably translated by Mr. Thompson. We shall be glad to receive more of that gentleman's publications, for good translation, whether from the French or any other language, is not too common amongst us. The publication is got up with the taste always displayed by the firm of Burns, Oates, and Co."—*Register.*

"The more we have of such works as 'The Hidden Life of Jesus,' the better."—*Westminster Gazette.*

"A book of searching power."—*Church Review.*

"We have often regretted that this writer's works are not better known."—*Universe.*

"We earnestly recommend its study and practice to all readers."—*Tablet.*

"We have to thank Mr. Thompson for this translation of a valuable work which has long been popular in France."—*Dublin Review.*

"A good translation."—*Month.*

BURNS, OATES, & CO., 63, PATERNOSTER ROW, E.C.

Devotion to the Nine Choirs of Holy Angels, and especially to the Angel Guardians. Translated from the Same. 3s.

" We congratulate Mr. Thompson on the way in which he h accomplished his task, and we earnestly hope that an increased devotion to the Holy Angels may be the reward of his labour of love."—*Tablet.*

" A beautiful translation."—*The Month.*

" The translation is extremely well done."—*Weekly Register.*

Library of Religious Biography. Edited by EDWARD HEALY THOMPSON.

Vol. 1. THE LIFE OF ST. ALOYSIUS GONZAGA, S.J. 5s.

" We gladly hail the first instalment of Mr. Healy Thompson's Library of Religious Biography. The life before us brings out strongly a characteristic of the Saint which is, perhaps, little appreciated by many who have been attracted to him chiefly by the purity and early holiness which have made him the chosen patron of the young. This characteristic is his intense energy of will, which reminds us of another Saint, of a very different vocation and destiny, whom he is said to have resembled also in personal appearance—the great St. Charles Borromeo."—*Dublin Review.*

" The book before us contains numberless traces of a thoughtful and tender devotion to the Saint. It shows a loving penetration into his spirit, and an appreciation of the secret motives of his action, which can only be the result of a deeply affectionate study of his life and character."—*Month.'*

Vol. 2. THE LIFE OF MARIE EUSTELLE HARPAIN; or, the Angel of the Eucharist. 5s.

"The life of Marie Eustelle Harpain possesses a special value and interest apart from its extraordinary natural and supernatural beauty, from the fact that to her example and to the effect of her writings is attributed in great measure the wonderful revival of devotion to the Blessed Sacrament in France, and consequently throughout Western Christendom."—*Dublin Review.*

" A more complete instance of that life of purity and close union with God in the world of which we have just been speak-

BURNS, OATES, & CO., 17, PORTMAN STREET, W.

ing is to be found in the history of Marie Eustelle Harpain, the sempstress of Saint-Pallais. The writer of the present volume has had the advantage of very copious materials in the French works on which his own work is founded, and Mr. Thompson has discharged his office as editor with his usual diligence and accuracy."—*The Month.*

Vol. 3. THE LIFE OF ST. STANISLAS KOSTKA. 5s.

"We strongly recommend this biography to our readers, earnestly hoping that the writer's object may thereby be attained in an increase of affectionate veneration for one of whom Urban VIII. exclaimed that, although 'a little youth,' he was indeed 'a great saint.'"—*Tablet.*

"There has been no adequate biography of St. Stanislas. In rectifying this want, Mr. Thompson has earned a title to the gratitude of English-speaking Catholics. The engaging Saint of Poland will now be better known among us, and we need not fear that, better known, he will not be better loved."—*Weekly Register.*

The Life of S. Teresa, written by herself: a new Translation from the last Spanish Edition. To which is added for the first time in English THE RELATIONS, or the Manifestations of her Spiritual State which the Saint submitted to her Confessors. Translated by DAVID LEWIS. In a handsome volume, 8vo, cloth, 10s. 6d.

"The work is incomparable; and Mr. Lewis's rare faithfulness and felicity as a translator are known so well, that no word of ours can be necessary to make the volume eagerly looked for."—*Dublin Review.*

"We have in this grand book perhaps the most copious spiritual autobiography of a Saint, and of a highly-favoured Saint, that exists."—*Month.*

The Life of Margaret Mary Alacoque. By the Rev. F. TICKELL, S.J. 8vo, cloth, 7s. 6d.

"It is long since we have had such a pleasure as the reading of Father Tickell's book has afforded us. No incident of her holy life from birth to death seems to be wanting, and the volume appropriately closes with an account of her beatification."—*Weekly Register*.

"It is one of those high-class spiritual biographies which will be best appreciated in religious communities." —*Westminster Gazette*.

"Of Father Tickell's labours we can say with pleasure that he has given us a real biography, in which the Saint is everything, and the biographer keeps in the background."—*Dublin Review*.

"We can only hope that the life may carry on, as it is worthy of doing, the apostolate begun in our country by one who our Lord desires should be 'as a brother to His servant, sharing equally in these spiritual goods, united with her to His own Heart for ever.'"—*Tablet*.

"The work could hardly have been done in a more unpretending, and at the same time more satisfactory, manner than in the volume now before us."—*Month*.

The Day Hours of the Church. Latin and English. Cloth, 1s.

Also, separately,

THE OFFICES OF PRIME AND COMPLINE. 8d.

THE OFFICES OF TIERCE, SEXT, AND NONE. 3d.

"Prime and Compline are the morning and evening prayers which the Church has drawn up for her children; and, for our part, we can wish for nothing better. We know not where an improvement could be suggested, and therefore we see not why anything should have been substituted for them. . . . Why should not their use be restored? Why should they not become the standard devotions of all Catholics, whether alone or in their families? Why may we not hope to have them more solemnly performed—chanted even every day in all religious communities; or, where there is a sufficient number of persons, even in family chapels?"—*Cardinal Wiseman*.

"These beautiful little books, which have received the imprimatur of his Grace the Archbishop, are a zealous priest's answers to the most eminent Cardinal's questions—such answers as would have gladdened his heart could they have been given when first demanded. But the Cardinal lives in his successors and what he so greatly desired should be done is in progress of full performance."—*Tablet.*

"The publication of these Offices is another proof of what we have before alluded to, viz., the increased liturgical taste of the present day."—*Catholic Opinion*

POPULAR DEVOTION.
Now ready.

Devotions for the Ecclesiastical Seasons, consisting of Psalms, Hymns, Prayers, &c., suited for Evening Services, and arranged for Singing. Cloth, 1s. Also in separate Nos. at 2d. each, for distribution, as follows:—

1. Advent and Christmas.
2. Septuagesima to Easter.
3. Paschal Time.
4. Whitsuntide.
5. Sundays after Pentecost.
6. Feasts of our Lady.
7. Saints' Days.

Music for the whole, 1s. 6d.

"A valuable addition to our stock of popular devotions."—*Dublin Review.*

Church Music and Church Choirs: 1. The Music to be Sung; 2. The proper Singers; 3. The Place for the Choir. 2s.

"The special value of this pamphlet, and the seasonableness of its circulation, lie in this: that it attempts to solve—and, we believe, does really solve—several important points as to the proper kinds of music to be used in our public Offices, and more especially at High Mass."—*Tablet.*

"We earnestly recommend all who can do so to procure and study this pamphlet."—*Weekly Register.*

"Masterly and exhaustive articles."—*Catholic Opinion.*

BURNS, OATES, & CO, 63, PATERNOSTER ROW, E.C.

Liturgical Directions for Organists, Singers, and Composers. Contains the Instructions of the Holy See on the proper kind of Music for the Church, from the Council of Trent to the present time; and thus furnishes choirs with a guide for selection. Fcp. 8vo, 6d.

New Meditations for each Day in the Year on the Life of our Lord Jesus Christ. By a Father of the Society of Jesus. With the imprimatur of his Grace the Archbishop of Westminster. Second Edition. Vols. I. and II., price 4s. 6d. each; or complete in two vols., 9s.

" We can heartily recommend this book for its style and substance; it bears with it several strong recommendations. . . . It is solid and practical without being dreary or commonplace." *Westminster Gazette.*

" A work of great practical utility, and we give it our earnest recommendation."—*Weekly Register.*

The Day Sanctified: being Meditations and Spiritual Readings for Daily Use. Selected from the Works of Saints and approved writers of the Catholic Church. Fcp., cloth, 3s. 6d.; red edges, 4s.

" Of the many volumes of meditation on sacred subjects which have appeared in the last few years, none has seemed to us so well adapted to its object as the one before us."—*Tablet.*

" Deserves to be specially mentioned."—*Month.*

"Admirable in every sense."—*Church Times.*

" Many of the Meditations are of great beauty. . . . They form, in fact, excellent little sermons, and we have no doubt will be largely used as such."—*Literary Churchman.*

BURNS, OATES, & CO., 17, PORTMAN STREET, W.

Our Father: Popular Discourses on the Lord's Prayer. By Dr. EMANUEL VEITH, Preacher in Ordinary in the Cathedral of Vienna. (Dr. V. is one of the most eminent preachers on the Continent.) Cloth, 3s. 6d.

" We can heartily recommend these as accurate, devotional, and practical."—*Westminster Gazette.*

" We are happy to receive and look over once more this beautiful work on the Lord's Prayer—most profitable reading."—*Weekly Register.*

" Most excellent manual."—*Church Review.*

Little Book of the Love of God. By Count STOLBERG. With Life of the Author. Cloth, 2s.

" An admirable little treatise, perfectly adapted to our language and modes of thought."—*Bishop of Birmingham.*

NEW BOOK FOR HOLY COMMUNION.

Reflections and Prayers for Holy Communion. Translated from the French. Uniform with " Imitation of the Sacred Heart." With Preface by Archbishop MANNING. Fcp. 8vo, cloth, 4s. 6d.; bound, red edges, 5s.; calf, 8s.; morocco, 9s.

" The Archbishop has marked his approval of the work by writing a preface for it, and describes it as ' a valuable addition to our books of devotion.' We may mention that it contains ' two very beautiful methods of hearing Mass,' to use the words of the Archbishop in the Preface."—*Register.*

" A book rich with the choicest and most profound Catholic devotions."—*Church Review.*

BURNS, OATES, & CO., 63, PATERNOSTER ROW, E.C.

Holy Confidence. By Father ROGACCI, of the Society of Jesus. One vol. 18mo, cloth, 2s.

" As an attack on the great enemy, despair, no work could be more effective; while it adds another to a stock of books of devotion which is likely to be much prized."—*Weekly Register.*

"This little book, addressed to those 'who strive to draw nearer to God and to unite themselves more closely with Him,' is one of the most useful and comforting that we have read for a long time. We earnestly commend this little book to all troubled souls, feeling sure that they will find in it abundant cause for joy and consolation."—*Tablet.*

The Invitation Heeded: Reasons for a Return to Catholic Unity. By JAMES KENT STONE, late President of Kenyon College, Gambier, Ohio, and of Hobart College. Cloth, 5s. 6d.

"A very important contribution to our polemical literature, which can hardly fail to be a standard work on the Anglican controversy."—*Dr. Brownson in the New York Tablet.*

₊ Of this able work 3000 have already been sold in America.

The New Testament Narrative, in the Words of the Sacred Writers. With Notes, Chronological Tables, and Maps. A book for those who, as a matter of education or of devotion, wish to be thoroughly well acquainted with the Life of our Lord. What is narrated by each of His Evangelists is woven into a continuous and chronological narrative. Thus the study of the Gospels is complete and yet easy. Cloth, 2s.

"The compilers deserve great praise for the manner in which they have performed their task. We commend this little volume as well and carefully printed, and as furnishing its readers, more-

BURNS, OATES, & CO., 17, PORTMAN STREET, W.

over, with a great amount of useful information in the tables inserted at the end."—*Month.*

" It is at once clear, complete, and beautiful."—*Catholic Opinion.*

Balmez: Protestantism and Catholicism compared in their Effects upon European Civilisation. Cloth, 7s. 6d.

∗⁎∗ A new edition of this far-famed Treatise.

The See of St. Peter. By T. W. ALLIES. A new and improved edition, with Preface on the present State of the Controversy. 4s. 6d.

Lallemant's Doctrine of the Spiritual Life. Edited by Dr. FABER. New Edition. Cloth, 4s. 6d.

"This excellent work has a twofold value, being both a biography and a volume of meditations. Father Lallemant's life does not abound with events, but its interest lies chiefly in the fact that his world and his warfare were within. His ' Spiritual Doctrine' contains an elaborate analysis of the wants, dangers, trials, and aspirations of the inner man, and supplies to the thoughtful and devout reader the most valuable instructions for the attainment of heavenly wisdom, grace, and strength."— *Catholic Times.*

" A treatise of the very highest value."—*Month.*

" The treatise is preceded by a short account of the writer's life, and has had the wonderful advantage of being edited by the late Father Faber."—*Weekly Register.*

" One of the very best of Messrs. Burns and Co.'s publications is this new edition of F. Lallemant's ' Spiritual Doctrine.' "— *Westminster Gazette.*

BURNS, OATES, & CO., 63, PATERNOSTER ROW, E.C.

The Rivers of Damascus and Jordan: a Causerie. By a Tertiary of the Order of St. Dominick. 4s.

"Good solid reading."—*Month.*
"Well done, and in a truly charitable spirit."—*Catholic Opinion.*
"It treats the subject in so novel and forcible a light, that we are fascinated in spite of ourselves, and irresistibly led on to follow its arguments and rejoice at its conclusions."—*Tablet.*

Eudoxia: a Tale of the Fifth Century. From the German of IDA, COUNTESS HAHN-HAHN. Cloth elegant, 4s.

"This charming tale may be classed among such instructive as well as entertaining works as 'Fabiola' and 'Callista.' It adds another laurel to the brow of the fair Countess."—*Weekly Register.*
"Instructive and interesting book."—*Northern Press.*

Tales for the Many. By CYRIL AUSTIN. In Five Numbers, at 2d. each; also, cloth, 1s.; gilt edges, 1s. 6d.

"Calculated to do good in our lending-libraries."—*Tablet.*
"We wish the volume all the success it deserves, and shall always welcome with pleasure any effort from the same quarter."—*Weekly Register.*
"One of the most delightful books which Messrs. Burns and Oates have brought out to charm children at this festive season."—*Catholic Opinion.*

In the Snow; or, Tales of Mount St. Bernard. By the Rev Dr. ANDERDON. Cloth neat, 3s. 6d.

"A collection of pretty stories."—*Star.*
"An excellent book for a present."—*Universe.*

BURNS, OATES, & CO., 17, PORTMAN STREET, W.

"A capital book of stories."—*Catholic Opinion*.
"An agreeable book."—*Church Review*.
"An admirable fireside companion."—*Nation*.
"A very interesting volume of tales."—*Freeman*.

"Several successive stories are related by different people assembled together, and thus a greater scope is given for variety, not only of the matter, but also the tone of each story, according to the temper and position of the narrators. Beautifully printed, tastefully bound, and reflects great credit on the publishers."

"A pleasing contribution."—*Month*.

"A charming volume. We congratulate Catholic parents and children on the appearance of a book which may be given by the former with advantage, and read by the latter with pleasure and edification."—*Dublin Review*.

By the same Author.

The Seven Ages of Clarewell: A History of a Spot of Ground. Cloth, 3s.

"We have an attractive work from the pen of an author who knows how to combine a pleasing and lively style with the promotion of the highest principles and the loftiest aims. The volume before us is beautifully bound, in a similar way to 'In the Snow,' by the same author, and is therefore very suitable for a present."—*Westminster Gazette*.

"A pleasing novelty in the style and character of the book, which is well and clearly sustained in the manner it is carried out."—*Northern Press*.

"Each stage furnishes the material for a dramatic scene; are very well hit off, and the whole makes up a graphic picture."—*Month*.

"'Clarewell' will give not only an hour of pleasant reading, but will, from the nature of the subject, be eminently suggestive of deep and important truths."—*Tablet*.

WORKS BY LADY GEORGIANA FULLERTON.

Life of Mary Fitzgerald, a Child of the Sacred Heart. Price 1s.; cloth extra, 2s.

WORKS BY LADY GEORGIANA FULLERTON (continued).

Rose Leblanc. A Tale of great interest. Cloth, 3s.

Grantley Manor. (The well-known and favourite Novel). Cloth, 3s.; cheap edition, 2s. 6d.

Life of St. Frances of Rome. Neat cloth, 2s. 6d.; cheap edition, 1s. 8d.

Edited by the Same.

Our Lady's Little Books. Neat cloth, 2s.; separate Numbers, 4d. each.

Life of the Honourable E. Dormer, late of the 60th Rifles. 1s.; cloth extra, 2s.

Helpers of the Holy Souls. 6d.

Tales from the Diary of a Sister of Mercy. By C. M. BRAME.

CONTENTS: The Double Marriage—The Cross and the Crown—The Novice—The Fatal Accident—The Priest's Death—The Gambler's Wife—The Apostate—The Besetting Sin.

Beautifully bound in bevelled cloth, 3s. 6d.

"Written in a chaste, simple, and touching style."—*Tablet.*

"This book is a casket; and those who open it will find the gem within."—*Register.*

"Calculated to promote the spread of virtue, and to check that of vice; and cannot fail to have a good effect upon all—young and old—into whose hands it may fall."—*Nation.*

"A neat volume, composed of agreeable and instructive tales.

Each of its tales concludes with a moral, which supplies food for reflection."—*Westminster Gazette.*

"They are well and cleverly told, and the volume is neatly got up."—*Month.*

"Very well told; all full of religious allusions and expressions."—*Star.*

"Very well written, and life-like—many very pathetic."—*Catholic Opinion.*

"An excellent work; reminds us forcibly of Father Price's 'Sick Calls.'"—*Universe.*

"A very interesting series of tales."—*Sun.*

By the Same.

Angels' Visits: A Series of Tales. With Frontispiece and Vignette. 3s. 6d.

"The tone of the book is excellent, and it will certainly make itself a great favourite with the young."—*Month.*

"Beautiful collection of Angel Stories. All who may wish to give any dear children a book which speaks in tones suited to the sweet simplicity of their innocent young hearts about holy things cannot do better than send for 'Angels' Visits.'"—*Weekly Register.*

"One of the prettiest books for children we have seen."—*Tablet.*

"A book which excites more than ordinary praise. We have great satisfaction in recommending to parents and all who have the charge of children this charming volume."—*Northern Press*

"A good present for children. An improvement on the 'Diary of a Sister of Mercy.'"—*Universe.*

"Touchingly written, and evidently the emanation of a refined and pious mind."—*Church Times.*

"A charming little book, full of beautiful stories of the family of angels."—*Church Opinion.*

"A nicely-written volume."—*Bookseller.*

"Gracefully-written stories."—*Star.*

Just out, ornamental cloth, 5s.

Legends of Our Lady and the Saints: or, Our Children's Book of Stories in Verse. Written

BURNS, OATES, & CO., 63, PATERNOSTER ROW, E.C.

for the Recitations of the Pupils of the Schools of the Holy Child Jesus, St. Leonards-on-Sea. Cheap Edition, 2s. 6d.

"It is a beautiful religious idea that is realised in the 'Legends of Our Lady and the Saints.' We are bound to add that it has been successfully carried out by the good nuns of St. Leonards. The children of their Schools are unusually favoured in having so much genius and taste exerted for their instruction and delight. The book is very daintily decorated and bound, and forms a charming present for pious children."—*Tablet.*

"The 'Legends' are so beautiful, that they ought to be read by all lovers of poetry."—*Bookseller.*

"Graceful poems."—*Month.*

Edith Sydney: a Tale of the Catholic Movement. By MISS OXENHAM. 5s.

"A novel for the novel-reader, and at the same time it is a guide to the convert and a help to their instructors."—*Universe.*

"Miss Oxenham shows herself to be a fair writer of a controversial tale, as well as a clever delineator of character."—*Tablet.*

"A charming romance. We introduce 'Edith Sydney' to our readers, confident that she will be a safe and welcome visitor in many a domestic circle, and will attain high favour with the Catholic reading public."—*Nation.*

"Miss Oxenham seems to possess considerable powers for the delineation of character and incident."—*Month.*

Not Yet: a Tale of the Present Time. By MISS OXENHAM. 5s.

"The lighter order of Catholic literature receives a very welcome addition in this story, which is original and very striking. The author is mistress of a style which is light and pleasant. The work is one to which we can give our heartiest commendation."—*Cork Examiner.*

"We are indebted to Miss Oxenham for one of the most interesting sensational Catholic tales yet published."—*Catholic Opinion.*

"Wholesome and pleasant reading, evincing a refined and cultivated understanding."—*Union Review.*

"Miss Oxenham's work would rank well even among Mudie's novels, although its one-volume form is likely to be unfavourable in the eyes of ordinary novel-readers; but, in nine cases out of ten, a novelette is more effective than a regular novel, and any more padding would have merely diluted the vivid and unflagging interest which the authoress of 'Not Yet' has imparted to her elegantly-bound volume. The plot is as original as a plot can be; it is well laid and carefully and ably worked out."—*Westminster Gazette.*

Nellie Netteville: a Tale of Ireland in the Time of Cromwell. By CECILIA CADDELL, Author of "Wild Times." 5s.; cheap edition, 3s. 6d.

"A very interesting story. The author's style is pleasing, picturesque, and good, and we recommend our readers to obtain the book for themselves."—*Church News.*

"A tale well told and of great interest."—*Catholic Opinion.*

"Pretty pathetic story—well told."—*Star.*

"Pretty book-history of cruelties inflicted by Protestant domination in the sister country—full of stirring and affecting passages."—*Church Review.*

"Tale is well told, and many of the incidents, especially the burning of the chapel with the priest and congregation by the Cromwellian soldiers, are intensely interesting."—*Universe.*

"By a writer well known, whose reputation will certainly not suffer by her new production."—*Month.*

Marie; or, the Workwoman of Liège. By CECILIA CADDELL. Cloth, 3s. 6d.

"This is another of those valuable works like that of 'Marie Eustelle Harpain.' Time would fail us were we to enumerate either her marvellous acts of charity, or the heroic sufferings she endured for the sake of others, or the wonderful revelations with which her faith and charity were rewarded."—*Tablet*.

"The author of 'Wild Times,' and other favourite works, is to be congratulated on the issue of a volume which is of more service than any book of fiction, however stirring. It is a beautiful work—beautiful in its theme and in its execution."—*Weekly Register*.

"Miss Caddell has given us a very interesting biography of 'Marie Sellier, the Workwoman of Liège,' known in the 17th century as 'Sœur Marie Albert.' Examples such as that so gracefully set forth in this volume are much needed among us."—*Month*.

The Countess of Glosswood: a Tale of the Times of the Stuarts. From the French. 3s. 6d.

"The tale is well written, and the translation seems cleverly done."—*Month*.

"This volume is prettily got up, and we can strongly recommend it to all as an excellent and instructive little book to place in the hands of the young."—*Westminster Gazette*.

"An excellent translation, and a very pretty tale, well told." —*Catholic Opinion*.

"This is a pretty tale of a Puritan conversion in the time of Charles II., prettily got up, and a pleasing addition to our lending-libraries."—*Tablet*.

"This tale belongs to a class of which we have had to thank Messrs. Burns for many beautiful specimens. Such books, while they are delightful reading to us who are happily Catholics, have another important merit—they set forth the claims of Catholicism, and must do a vast deal of good among Protestants who casually meet with and peruse them. The book before us is beautifully got up, and would be an ornament to any table."—*Weekly Register*.

BURNS, OATES, & CO., 17, PORTMAN STREET, W.

www.ingramcontent.com/pod-product-compliance
Lightning Source LLC
Chambersburg PA
CBHW022131160426

43197CB00009B/1243